POWERS OF THE ORISHAS

ORISHAS

Santería and
The Worship of Saints

POWERS OF THE ORISHAS

Santería and
The Worship of Saints

By
Migene González-Wippler

Original Publications
New York

POWERS OF THE ORISHAS
By Migene Gonzalez Wippler
ISBN: 0-942272-25-0

Copyright © 1992 Original Publications

Cover art by Raul Canizares

Original Publications
P.O. Box 236
Old Bethpage, New York 11804-0236

Printed in the United States of America

*This book is dedicated to the memory of
Eduardo Pastoriza — Chango Larí*

Eleggua agui Iboru Ibolla Aguibochiche.
Orunla oya ofoillo oloae acatasorda alamanibata
odoribale jicoyeru adobire allaguna aforibi
apapa orobisilio y unsolellu. Oggun aguaniye oke,
Ochosi odemata matasi, Osun malabure labosun Orunla ashé . . .

Preface

▼▼▼

After my sixth book on Santería was published, (*Santería: The Religion*), Harmony Books, 1989, I decided I had completed my work on the subject. Not that I had exhausted the topic. Santería is a very complex religion and very many volumes must be written before most of its mysteries are revealed. I say most, and not all, because like other mystery religions the keys to Santería lie in many hands and in many traditions. No one has all the answers nor all the knowledge that encompasses it. I have been researching and studying Santería for nearly twenty years, and I feel as if I were still scratching the surface. Many of the hundreds of sources I have tapped in my work are at odds with each other. Many of the priests and priestesses of the religion —babalawos, oriatés, iyalochas and babalochas — do not agree on all the practices and beliefs of Santería.

There are disagreements on everything: from the true names of the orishas or saints to their relationship between themselves, the various legends or patakis and the appropriate offerings and rituals. In the face of such disparity, the interested student must exercise both prudence and good judgment if the truth, at least some of it, is to be gleaned. To add to the problem, the elders are loth to part with any of the secrets of the religion. They even keep their own initiates — *ahijados* — in the dark about some of the rituals and *ebbós*. Why? Because Santería began in secrecy, to protect its practices from the persecution of the Spanish colonists. And today, when secrecy is no longer necessary, tradition demands its preservation.

In order to learn more about the intricacies of the religion many researchers resort to undergo some of its initiations. But the santeros are aware of such practices, and as a result do not reveal any major secrets, even if they accede to give the initiations. An outsider may receive the necklaces or the Warriors, but they will not be told how they are prepared. Even when a person goes all the way and "makes the saint," becoming a santero in the process, he or she will not be informed of any ritualistic secrets or preparations. That person will have to learn through a long process of observation, long enough to discourage anyone who is simply curious about the religion. I know more than one initiated santero who knows next to nothing about the practices of Santería. Those persons were initiated into the religion, and then the officiating santero or "padrino" withdrew, leaving them to their own devices. This was the padrino's way to protect his religion from someone whom he considered not to be sincere in his or her involvement. If the person was indeed sincere, he or she would find a way to learn how to practice Santería. If not, the door to the mysteries was effectively shut.

My own interest in Santería is both serious and genuine. I believe it is a fascinating religion worthy of thorough study, particularly in the way it impacts on the Latin American communities and the psychological effects it has on its practitioners. In recent years increasing numbers of researchers, particularly those in the fields of psychiatry, anthropology and sociology, have devoted much serious work to the subject of Santería. This is an excellent trend, which I hope will continue to grow.

Why did I decide to write another book on Santería? Because I wanted to clarify some things and add some others to what I had already said. In all likelihood, this will be the last book I write on the subject, but I'm not making any promises. There is still so very much to learn.

Migene González-Wippler
New York City

Contents

The Practice of
Santería

▼▼▼

Santería is an Afro-Cuban religion based on an amalgamation between some of the magico-religious beliefs and practices of the Yoruba people and those of the Catholic church. In Cuba, where the Yoruba proliferated extensively, they became known as *Lucumí*, a word that means "friendship." Some authorities believe that the word *Lucumí* is derived from *akumi*, which means *I am Aku*, a term that describes the Yoruba in Sierra Leone.

Santería is known in Cuba as *la religión Lucumí*, that is, the *Lucumí* religion. The original Yoruba language, interspersed with Spanish terms and corrupted through centuries of misuse and mispronunciation, also became known as *Lucumí*. Today most of the *Lucumí* terms used in Santería would not be recognized as Yoruba in Southwestern Nigeria, the country of origin of the Yoruba people.

Santería is a Spanish term that means a confluence of saints and their worship. These saints are in reality clever disguises for some of the Yoruba deities, known as orishas. During the slave trade, the Yorubas who were brought to Cuba were forbidden the practice of their religion by their Spanish masters. In order to continue their magical and religious observances safely the slaves opted for the identification and disguise of the orishas with some of the Catholic saints worshipped by the Spaniards. In this manner they were able to worship their deities under the very noses of the Spaniards without danger of punishment. The same syncretic phenomenon took place in Brazil where the new religion thus born became known as Candomble and Macumba.

Throughout the centuries the practices of the Yorubas —now known as *Lucumí* — became very popular and soon many of the Creoles, who were descendants of the Spaniards, began to practice the new religion. They became known as santeros or santeras, who are the priests and priestesses of Santería. The saints/orishas or Santería are identified with natural forces, as well as with human interests or endeavors. These deities have also been anthropomorphized so that each one has been imbued with intensely human characteristics that make them very real to the practitioners and easy to identify with. In most cases, the orishas have many aspects or paths. In each aspect the deity has a different set of qualities and traits, although remaining true to his/her identity. That makes it easier to find correlations between the deity and their "children," who are those persons who fall under their direct influence. According to a central belief of Santería, every human being is ruled by one of the orishas/saints in a specific aspect of that deity. It does not matter whether the person believes in Santería.

Contrary to what many people believe, Santería is neither a sect nor a cult. It is a monotheistic religion, where God is seen as the Creator of the universe and of humanity. The orishas, syncretized with Catholic saints, are repositories of God's powers and the mediators between humanity and the Supreme Being.

God in Santería is known as Olodumare. Humanity's personal God — an aspect of Olodumare — is known as Olofi. The power of God — Olodumare — is cosmic energy, the stuff from which the universe was created. This power is known as *ashé*. Although there is only one kind of ashé, it can be expressed or manifested in many different ways. Each orisha/saint has the capacity to manipulate this energy and use it in his or her own special sphere of influence. The orisha Oshún, identified with Our Lady of La Caridad del Cobre, manifests her ashé as love and the capacity to bring about union between two people. She can also transform ashé into gold, which is another of her attributes.

The main purpose of the practitioners of Santería is to

acquire ashé in order to achieve their desires. To get ashé it is necessary to give *ebbó* — an offering — to the orisha who controls the object of one's desires. An ebbó may be a cleansing, an offer of fruits or the orisha's favorite foods, and — in extreme cases —an animal sacrifice. The practice of animal sacrifices has given Santería much undeserved negative publicity. The majority of the animals sacrificed — most of them chickens and roosters — are eaten by the santeros after their rituals. Those which are not eaten are used during rubbing rituals to "cleanse" an individual of illnesses or what are considered dangerous vibrations. At no time do the santeros engage in sinister practices, such as human sacrifices. On the other hand, the santeros do not believe in conducting animal sacrifices routinely. According to Santería's beliefs the orishas become "heated" and displeased when animals are given often and indiscriminately. Therefore the most common offerings are fruits and favorite foods. Only when the orisha demands it or accepts it is an animal sacrifice given. This usually happens when a person's life is believed to be in jeopardy. But the orisha must approve the sacrifice before it can be offered.

In order to ascertain the will of an orisha/saint, Santería uses several divination systems. There are four basic divinations:

1. *The coconut shells, also known as Obi,* where four pieces of coconut are used to question an orisha. This system is most commonly used to ask an orisha if he/she is pleased with an offer. It is not used often to query the orishas. Anyone may use this system, but the santeros recommend that the person receive the initiation known as Eleggua and the Warriors before attempting to read the coconut. But one does not have to be an initiated priest or santero to use this system of divination.

2. *The cowrie shells, also known as the Diloggún or Caracoles.* This system employs 16 shells and is the

most common of the divinations. It should only be used by initiated priests and requires many years of study before any degree of proficiency may be reached. The santeros — alternately known as *babalochas* (the men) and *iyalochas* (the women) — who become proficient at reading the Diloggún become known as *Italeros*. An *itá* is a life-time reading of the Diloggún. Those priests who are very knowledgeable in the religion and the Diloggún can become Oriatés. These are the priests who officiate during the initiation ceremonies.

3. *The Okuelé*, a divining chain used by the babalawos who are the high priests of Santería. The okuelé consists of eight medallions usually made of coconut shells.

4. *The Table of Ifá* or *Opón Ifá*, which is the Oracle of Santería. This is the highest divination system of the religion and is used only by the babalawos during their ritual ceremonies or when they are determining who is the ruling orisha of an individual.

The Caracoles or Diloggún is the most widely used of the divination systems. When the cowrie shells are thrown by the santero or Oriaté on their working table, the shells can fall in one of several patterns or *oddus*. Each oddu has a name and a number. Several of the orishas are said to "speak" through the patterns or oddus. The santero throws the shells several times to determine the will of the orishas and how he can best help his client. The first two times he throws the shells he obtains two numbers. This double digit has a proverb that is applied to the person's problem and is interpreted accordingly. There are also prescribed ebbós connected to each oddu, and several legends that describe many of the cosmic events surrounding the lives of the orishas. These legends are known as *patakis*.

Each of the orishas owns a set of 18 cowrie shells, except Eleggua who owns 21. The cowries are part of the major initiation of Santería, which is known as the *asiento*. Although the orishas own 18 cowries, only 16 of those are read in the Diloggún. The santero usually reads the cowrie shells that belong to Eleggua. Only when a specific orisha has to be queried for a special reason are his or her shells read.

Whenever a person wishes to determine his ruling orisha, he may find out either through the babalawo or the oriaté. The babalawo uses the Table of Ifá to find this out. The oriaté uses the Diloggún, but instead of reading them on his working table, he reads them on a straw mat known as an *estera*. The mat is placed on the floor where the oriaté proceeds with the reading. In Spanish this is known as *bajar el caracol a la estera*.

The santeros say that "el santo," that is, the secrets of the saints, are composed of four things: water, herbs, cowrie shells and stones. They refer to the main ingredients necessary to conduct the asiento ceremony, when a person becomes a priest or priestess of the religion. With herbs (known as *ewe*) and water they prepare a liquid known as *omiero*, which is used to wash all the working implements of the saints or orishas. The stones, known as *otanes*, are said to be the embodiment of the orishas, while the cowries are the mouthpieces of the deities.

The practice of Santería is based on progressive initiations. The two basic initiations are:

1. The *Necklaces* or *Elekes*, where the initiate undergoes a one-day ceremony during which he receives the bead necklaces of the five major orishas. These are Eleggua, Obatalá, Changó, Yemayá and Oshún. The necklaces are said to be the banners of the saints and protect their owners against many dangers.

2. Eleggua and the Warriors (Los Guerreros), where the initiate receives the cement head that represents the powerful orisha known as Eleggua, as well as a cauldron with the working implements of two warrior orishas known as Oggún and Ochosi. The initiate also receives a small cup surmounted by a metal rooster and several tiny bells known as Osun. Eleggua and the Warriors help the person win many of life's battles, while Osun warns when danger is near. Together with the Necklaces this initiation is known as the foundation of Santería.

After receiving these two initiations, the practitioner may receive others, such as Olokun, the Icofá or Hand of Orúnla, and Orisha-Oko, without becoming a santero. Should he decide to become a priest or priestess, he/she must undergo the ceremony of the asiento, also known as *Kariocha*. The ceremony lasts seven days, at the end of which the oriaté and the santeros present conduct the ritual known as Itá, when the initiate receives a life reading and is told which of the higher initiations he must also undertake. After the asiento is over, the initiate must undergo an apprenticeship period that lasts one year and seven days. During this time he/she must dress in white and follow blindly the directions of his "padrino" or "madrina," who is the priest or priestess who initiated him/her in the mysteries of his/her ruling orisha.

During the asiento the initiate, known now as *yawó*, receives the mysteries of his orisha. This ceremony is conducted directly over the head of the yawó, who is said to be "crowned" by his saint. This crown is drawn on the yawó's shaven head and consists of a series of concentric circles using the four initiatory colors of Santería. These colors are white, red, blue and yellow. All the orishas share the colors, except Oshún who is the only one entitled to use the color yellow, a right granted to her directly by Olodumare himself. Each orisha has his/her own design, where the colors are placed in specific circles and combinations. The design is known as the "signature" of an orisha.

The implements and secrets of the orishas are given to the

yawó in fancy tureens in the colors of the orishas. Regardless of the orisha into whose mysteries he has been initiated, the yawó also receives the tureens or receptacles of Obatalá, Changó, Yemayá and Oshún. On the third day of the asiento, the yawó usually celebrates his induction as a priest with a *Tambor*, or drum party in honor of his orisha. During the Tambor, the sacred drums of Santería, known as the *Batáa*, are played. These drums are known as *Iyá, Itótele* and *Okónkolo*. Sometimes, when the Batáa are not available, a *Guiro* is played instead. During a Guiro only one drum is played, accompanied by two *shékeres*, or beaded gourds. During the playing, the yawó sits underneath a palium made with luxurious satin hangings. The palium is known as the yawó's "throne," and he sits there in the splendid regalia of his orisha, usually satin and brocade, ornamented with lace and cowrie shells. At his feet are all the barbarous implements of his orisha and the tureens containing the stones of the various deities. A vast offering of fruits, cakes, special foods and flowers complete the display. Those present at the Tambor pay their respects to the yawó. If they are priests or priestesses, they must salute by laying on the floor, face down if their ruling orisha is male, and sitting sideways, first on the left and then on the right, if their orisha is female. The yawó answers the greeting by laying down at the feet of the priest to receive his blessing. The priest does this by crossing his hands over the back of the yawó, tapping his shoulders lightly and muttering, *Awawató*, adding the name of the yawó's orisha. The yawó then rises and embraces the priest, touching shoulders, first the left, then the right, in the typical embrace of Santería. Those who are not priests salute by crossing their arms in front of their chests and bowing to the yawó, who repeats the gesture. Once everyone has saluted the yawó, they proceed to enjoy the Tambor, dancing to the drum rhythms that are played in honor of the various orishas. Very often during a Tambor, one or more of the orishas take possession of one or several of their initiates. It is during possession that the orishas speak directly. To be witness to a genuine possession — for there *are* bogus ones — is a startling experience. A person possessed by an orisha displays unusual strength and extraordinary powers of precognition and telepathy, indicating the release of vast amounts of psychic energy from the deep unconscious which remain just below the surface of the conscious personality without intruding in its normal functions. The drum rhythms, the chanting and the dancing seem to be directly conducive to the state of possession, suggesting the possibility of self-hypnosis as a precursor to the trance state. The fact that anyone, even the uninitiated, can fall into trance during a Tambor, seems to strengthen this hypothesis.

The purpose of this book is to present the major orishas of Santería in their syncretic identifications with some of the Catholic saints. The book has been divided into sections, rather than chapters, and each section deals with a specific orisha, the attributes, paths or aspects, necklaces, initiations, foods, herbs, legends, ebbós, and other pertinent information about that particular deity. This will allow the reader to glean as much data as possible about each orisha in a capsule form. Regrettably, not all the deities worshipped in Santería could be included in this small volume. Therefore some of the major orishas, such as Obba, Oddúa, Yewá, and Orisha-Oko were not presented in detail. This was not a deliberate omission, but rather a necessary one. These and the less known orishas are nevertheless a vital part of Santería, and those who are seriously interested in the religion should make every effort to learn more about them. Fortunately, in recent years there has been a growing academic interest in Santería and the result has been a series of highly informative and important books on the subject. The reader is encouraged to read them and to continue his search for additional information about this important syncretic religion.

Olodumare/Olofi

▼▼▼

The Yorubas, upon whose mythology are largely based in the magico-religious practices of Santería, believe in one supreme being known as Olodumare. This is God in a purely cosmic sense. As I mentioned before, all the orishas or deities are the repositories of Olodumare's power or energy, known as ashé. The Yorubas also believe in certain divinities or spirits, among whom are Obatalá (Orisanlá), Orúnmila (Orúnla), Odduduwa, Eshu (Eleggua) and Oggún; deified ancestors, such as Changó and Orisha-Oko; and personifications of natural forces such as Yemayá (the sea in Santería), Oshún (river waters), and the wind (Oyá). In Nigeria, Yemayá, Oshún and Oyá are also identified with the Oggún river, the Oshún river and the Niger river, respectively.

Olodumare is the creator. As such, he is unique, immortal, omnipotent, omniscient and transcendental. He is also king and judge of all that exists.

The Yorubas attach great significance to names and titles. For that reason, they have given God/Olodumare many names. Among these names are Olorún, which means the owner of heaven above. The Yorubas usually refer to the Supreme Being as Olorún Olodumare, meaning The Lord whose abode is in the heaven above. Another name given to Olodumare is Eledaa, meaning the Creator. This title implies that Olodumare is the source of all the creation.

Among the other titles given to Olodumare are Elemi, meaning the Owner of Life; Alaaye, the Living One; and Olojo Oni, the controller of daily happenings. Olofi, most commonly used in Santería to represent humanity's personal god, is a Yoruba divinity associated with the protection of crops. In Santería, God, the Creator, is seen as Olodumare. Eledaa is identified with each person's guardian angel. Olorún is God in heaven, identified with the sun. The babalawos, who are the high priests of Santería, salute the sun every morning with arms widespread and the palms of the hands uppermost. One of the initiations given by the babalawos, the Icofá or Hand of Orúnla, includes a beautiful ceremony to Olorún whose details cannot be revealed by the initiates. Alaaye, Elemi and Oloyo Oni are not revered in Santería. But undeniably, God on earth is Olofi, and that is the aspect of the Supreme Being the believers of Santería worship most commonly.

Olofi is not propitiated directly, as he is believed to be in too exalted a position, but the babalawos sometimes receive his mysteries in a very complex ceremony. Not all babalawos undergo this initiation, which is the highest to which they can aspire.

Olofi is syncretized as Jesus Christ. He is mentioned in every prayer and is highly revered, but is not appealed to in cases of need, as he has relegated all earthly matters to the attention of the orishas, who are his children and the intermediaries between him and humanity.

Eleggua

▼▼▼

SYNCRETISM OR IDENTIFICATION: Saint Anthony of Padua, the Holy Infant of Atocha and the Lonely Spirit (Anima Sola)

Eleggua and all the other orishas have many paths or aspects, which are known in Santería as *avatars*. As we will see in this section, Eleggua has 101 paths, of which 21 are most commonly used. In each path, the orisha is syncretized with a different Catholic saint. Thus there are at least 21 saints with which Eleggua has been identified. Among these are Saint Benito and Saint Martin of Porres. All the other orishas in their various paths have also been syncretized with more than one Catholic saint.

Saint Anthony of Padua — Feast Day: June 13th

This beloved saint is one of the great doctors of the Catholic Church. He was born in Lisbon, of a wealthy family in 1195 AD and died near Padua on June 13, 1231. His real name was Fernando but he changed it to Anthony when he took holy orders. He was a canon regular until the age of 25 in his native Portugal, but desiring to be a missionary, he joined the Franciscan order which sent him to work among the Muslims in Morocco. But his health, which was always frail, betrayed him and he had to return to Europe where he was for a time at a hermitage near Forli in Italy. Later he was sent to Padua where he spent the rest of his life. His extraordinary gift for preaching and his vast knowledge of Biblical scripture made him famous during his lifetime. Many miracles were ascribed to him while he was still living, and when he died at the untimely age of 36, he was already believed to be a saint. Among his acknowledged powers are the retrieving of lost things, the unification of lovers and spouses and the control over thieves. He also protects small children and is a champion of the poor, whose bread he procures. His identification with Eleggua is linked to the orisha's predilection for children, his involvement with stolen things and his great love of justice.

The Holy Infant of Atocha — Feast Day: January 1st

The story behind this saint is as follows. In the city of Atocha, in Spain, many Christians had been imprisoned during the last years of the Moorish occupation. The only people who could enter the prisons were children. One day a small child appeared at one of the prisons, with a large basket of bread and a pail of water. The moors were astounded when they saw that although many prisoners had eaten from the bread and drank from the water the basket was still overflowing with bread and the pail was still full of water. The child then disappeared. The story of this seeming miracle spread like wildfire throughout Spain, giving birth to the belief that the Christ child has taken compassion on the prisoners and had come down to earth to alleviate their suffering. This was how the belief in the Holy Infant of Atocha was born. Again, there is bread and the consolation of the poor in this story, as in that of Saint Anthony. The link with Eleggua is traced to the fact that the orisha is very fond of children and often manifests as one. He is also concerned with providing for human needs.

The Lonely Spirit — Feast Day: November 2nd

This is a representation of the souls who are in purgatory. The Lonely Spirit is one of these desperate souls, who are being purified in the eternal flames, waiting for the moment when they will be released from their suffering and join the souls of the elect in heaven. This spirit is used in magical works, as it will accede to work with humans in order to get their help in shortening its time in purgatory. This is allegedly possible through the giving of candles and prayers to the Lonely Spirit in exchange for its help in human affairs. The link with Eleggua is traced to the orisha's penchant to work on his own and his acceptance of offers in exchange for his help. Eleggua is quite capable of doing things which are mischievous, and in one of his aspects is affiliated with the spirits of the dead and cemeteries.

ELEGGUA AS A COSMIC FORCE

He is the opener of the doors; the messenger of the gods; he is a great diviner who does not need an oracle to see the future; he owns the keys to all doors, and to evil as well as to good; he seems to take pleasure in creating compromising situations and trouble between human beings; he can be equally cruel and generous; he is the unexpected, treacherous and dangerous and capricious like fate itself; he is the great justice wielder and though he may seem at times a master of deceit and the bringer of misfortune, his actions are always justified because he alone knows the true meaning of justice and sees things which are hidden from humanity, as well as from the other orishas. In other words, Eleggua can be equally identified with both fate and justice. It is said of this orisha that he's the lowest and the highest, a prince and a pauper who is equally at ease in a palace and a garbage dump, where he often feasts. With Oyá, he rules over the four winds. He is a great healer and a master magician. His spells and amulets are all powerful and impossible to destroy.

ELEGGUA'S REPRESENTATION

In Santería Eleggua is envisioned as a young, light-skinned mulatto, of a pleasant countenance, slim and agile. He is dressed in breeches and a cassock, in red and black. He wears a straw hat and a large knapsack by the side, filled with candies and all sorts of tricks. He carries a whistle around his neck and many bells and other noise makers. On one hand he carries a forked branch he uses to ensnare the unwary. The branch is painted in red and black. He is most commonly represented as a cement head with the eyes and mouth formed with cowrie shells. But in some of his aspects or paths he may be prepared inside a large seashell, a porous sea stone or a coconut.

ATTRIBUTES

A forked tree branch, painted red and black; a whistle; the cement head that represents him with cowrie shells for eyes and mouth; a straw hat; a set of 21 cowrie shells, a small black stone and an elongated sea shell, all of which are used in divination. Eleggua's Diloggún is the one most commonly used by the Santero and the oriaté (expert diviner) to consult their clients and to determine a person's ruling orisha.

Colors: Red and black

Day of the Week: Monday and the 3rd of each month

Number: 3, 21

Offerings: Toys, keys, a straw hat, mouse traps, guns and rifles, coconuts, candies, toasted corn, whistles, forked branches, rum, cigars and candles.

Necklace: Alternating red and black beads

Foods: Toasted corn, smoked fish and possum, palm oil *(manteca de corojo)*, fruits, all types of candies and cakes, male chickens, roosters, coconut, corn meal balls with honey and palm oil.

Herbs (in Spanish): Abre camino, almácigo, espartillo, guayabo, lengua de vaca, mastuerzo, pata de gallina, pica pica, rompezaraguey, llamao, hedionda, jobo, and many others.

ELEGGUA AS AN ARCHETYPE

As a human archetype Eleggua is identified as someone with mischievous tendencies, good humored and kind, a prankster, fond of playing jokes. He is said to be the master of lies and arbiter of truth, the father of traps and snares. His children are intelligent, but sometimes unscrupulous and given to intrigues.

PATHS OF ELEGGUA

Among the Yorubas Eleggua is known as Eshu and is one of the most revered and powerful of all the orishas. In Brazilian Candomblé he is also known as Eshu and identified loosely with the devil. This is altogether an erroneous concept, as Eleggua/Eshu is beyond good and evil. Furthermore, the devil is a Christian concept that does not exist among the Yorubas, who do not believe in totally opposing forces such as good and evil. Eleggua/Eshu works directly with Olodumare to test and try out the human spirit and help human beings along their evolutionary paths. One of his main concerns is the enforcement of the divine will and the punishment of those who choose to ignore the cosmic laws.

In Santería Eleggua/Eshu is said to have 101 "paths" or manifestations, but of these, 21 are the best known. In each path the name Eshu precedes the title that describes the path. The santeros say that there are seven types of Eleggua, and each of these has three paths. Together they make up the 21 paths which are the following:

Eshu Añiki —This represents the mother of all the Elegguas, as the orisha has several female aspects. She has three paths and in one of them she is shown with two faces. From her relationship with Eshu Ocuboro was born the Prince Elegbara or Eleggua. She heals with plants and uncovers all secrets. She governs the other Eshus and assigns their work. All the 21 Eshus form Eleggua.

Eshu Laroye — This Eshu is a close friend of Oshún and is the one who lives behind the door in a clay vessel. He is fond of candles, rum and toys and is playful and malicious and a great protector of the home. He is the Eleggua identified with Saint Anthony of Padua.

Eshu Alagwanna — This Eshu lives in the depths of the forests. He has a treaty with the *eggun*, who are the spirits of the dead, and is said to represent misfortune and hopelessness and to punish callousness and impiety. He sometimes stands at the crossroads where he may cause death through fire or knife wounds. This is the Eleggua who is identified with the Lonely Spirit.

Eshu Kilalu — Very little is known of this path.

Eshu Barakikeño — This Eshu is represented as a very young child, very mischievous who causes a great deal of trouble with his very presence.

Eshu Ocuboro — This is an oba (king) who is the father of Elegbara. He is said to have total power over life and death.

Eshu Afrá — This Eshu comes from the land of Arará (Dahomey) and "walks" with Babalú-Ayé. His necklace is made of alternating black and white beads. He is fond of whistling in the corners and in lonely places, and hates rum and palm wine.

Eshu Mikke — This Eshu likes to hide things and brandishes fire.

Eshu Bi — This Eshu lives in the street corners and is a warrior orisha who causes many types of accidents.

Eshu Tulu — Very little is known of this path.

Eshu Agosolé — Very little is known of this path, except that he is often used to prevent entrapments and deceit.

Eshu Alabode — Very little is known of this path.

Eshu Beleke — This Eshu is represented as a very young child, very clever and skillful who is an excellent guardian of the home. He is a great master of herbal remedies and takes part in every thing that happens in a house. He is said to be very jealous and should not be kept in homes with small children. It is this Eleggua who has been identified with the Holy Infant of Atocha.

Eshu Onibode — This Eshu acts as a guardian of the doors of both houses and cities. He is always placed outside the home so he will protect it better. He carries arrows and two keys. He is represented as a full figure, sitting down with 17 cowrie shells encrusted all over his head and four cowries to represent his eyes and ears. He wears a necklace tied around his neck.

Eshu Myulu, Eshu Otole, Eshu Miwa, Eshu Osika, Eshu Araibode, Eshu Yemi, and Eshu Ocholoforo are some of the lesser known aspects of Eleggua and very little is known about them.

Also very important, although not included in the 21 paths, are Eshu Ayé — who is prepared inside a large seashell and "walks" with Yemayá/Olokun — and Eshu Elufé, who is the oldest, and represented as an ancient old man, very strict and puritanical. Eshu Ogguanilebbe "walks" with Oggún and causes accidents and derailments and all sorts of tragedies. Eleggua Alalú Banché is the owner and lord of every situation and possibility, and has Olodumare's ashé to either solve problems or make them worse. For that reason he is the first to be honored in every ceremony. Eshu Afrodi and Eshu Agroi are from the land of Arará and each has 24 paths. They are decorated with 24 cowries placed along three lines. They are prepared in a pyramidal shape and are allied with Orúnmila. Only men can officiate in their ceremonies. As we can see, Eshu is the incarnation of all the evils that may affect humanity, although in some aspects he also provides the cure for these ills. He is not evil but represents the evil in the world of matter. Eleggua is a symbol of the positive and Eshu is a symbol of the negative in humanity. This duality of the orisha makes him difficult to understand but his importance is primordial in all human affairs. He stands at the door to the home because the interior of each home represents safety while the exterior represents danger. Well propitiated and understood, he will keep this danger away and preserve the safety of the home.

Eleggua is identified with Fate. He is the unknown, the unexpected. He brings about all changes, sometimes good and sometimes bad. His character is ambiguous. That is why his colors are red and black; red to symbolize life and black to symbolize death.

ELEGGUA AND THE WARRIORS

This initiation is one of the foundations of Santería and, together with the Necklaces, forms what is known by the santeros as a *medio asiento*, half of the major initiation known as the "asiento," when a person becomes a santero or santera.

Eleggua and the Warriors are given to a person as a protection against the battles of life. The initiation includes the conferring of the powers of Eleggua — symbolized by the cement head that represents him — and those of Oggún and Ochosi. The protective powers of Osun — who represents life itself — are also given in this initiation. Oggún is represented by the seven work implements associated with him, such as a rake, a hammer, an anvil and a saw. Ochosi is represented by a bow and arrow. These implements are placed inside a black cauldron. Osun is represented by a small metal rooster atop a cup framed by several tiny bells.

The initiation known as Eleggua and the Warriors is not to be confused with the initiation of Eleggua himself, when a person receives the mysteries of the orisha during the ceremony of the asiento. During that lengthy ritual, the initiate or yawó, is "crowned" with the ashé, the powers of Eleggua and becomes a priest or priestess of the orisha.

Both the santeros and the babalawos give Eleggua and the Warriors, but women should not attempt to give this initiation unless they have the help of a man in the preparation of Eleggua's head. The reason for this taboo is that Eleggua and the Warriors gather some of the virility of the man who prepares them in order to function properly.

THE LEGEND/PATAKI

Eleggua (Eshu) originates in the Yoruba city of Ketu in Nigeria, where he is believed to have been king. That is why he is also known as Eshu Alaketu. The legends or patakis of Santería are an intrinsic part of the divination systems that are at the core of the religion. As we have seen, among the divination systems are the reading of the coconut rinds; the cowrie shells — also known as the Diloggún; the okuelé or divining chain of the babalawo; and the Table of Ifá — Opón Ifá — which is the divining tray of the babalawo and the highest oracle in Santería. The oracle of Ifá — both the okuelé and the tray — and the cowrie shells or Diloggún are the greatest source of the legends or patakis. Each pattern of the Diloggún, the okuelé or the Opón Ifá is known as an oddu. Each oddu (256 in each oracle) is accompanied by several legends. These legends explain the origins of the orishas, the creation of the world and many of the mysteries of the religion. Each oddu is a mouthpiece for several of the orishas and is also accompanied by a rather cryptic aphorism, which the diviner uses to interpret the oracle. The oddu also has a vast quantity of ebbós which offer magical solutions for the problems faced by the consultant.

There are many patakis explaining the origin of Eleggua and his connection with Olodumare and with the other orishas. The most popular pataki tells the story of the Prince Elegbara (Eleggua), son of Ocuboro and Añiqui. One day he saw a great light with three eyes outside the palace. He approached the strange object and saw that it was a dry coconut. He picked it up and brought it to the palace where he threw it behind a door where it continued to shine. Three days later the prince died. At first, the king and his people continued to revere the shining coconut (obi), but in time they forgot about it. Shortly after this, the country suffered a reversal and poverty and despair reigned everywhere. The king gathered the elders to find out what was ailing his kingdom and after much deliberation, they determined that all their ills were caused by their abandonment of the obi. When they went to look at the coconut they found that it had rotten and was covered with worms. In order to make amends, they threw away the obi and replaced it with a stone which they put behind the door. This is the origin of Eleggua and the reason why he is placed behind the doors.

Another pataki tells how one day Olodumare became gravely ill and none of the orishas could cure him. Eleggua, who was very young, was not taken into consideration by the elder deities. When he learned that Olodumare was ailing he came to see the Creator and asked to be allowed to attempt a cure. The elder orishas laughed at him, but Olodumare silenced them and ordered them to step aside and let the young Eleggua do his thing. Eleggua reached into the knapsack that always hangs on his side and pulled out a few herbs. He quickly prepared a steaming brew and gave it to Olodumare to drink. As soon as the Creator drank the concoction he was healed of his illness. He immediately called all the orishas to his presence and proclaimed that from that day on Eleggua was to be the first to be honored in all their ceremonies. He also gave the young orisha the keys to all the doors and gave him the power of life and death and the grace to solve all problems. Knowing Eleggua's great sense of justice he also made him the arbiter of the affairs of humanity and the master of its fate.

THE ODDU

In the Diloggún, the oddus or patterns through which Eleggua speaks are called Okanasorde, Oggunda, Oddi and Ojuani, with the numbers 1, 3, 7 and 11 respectively.

RULERSHIP

Eleggua is known as the man of the crossroads. He protects

against the machinations of enemies, against altercations, treason, deceit, accidents, blood disorders, sorrows and poverty. He can change the worst luck into the best and vice versa. He is a champion of the poor and the desolate and is the worst enemy of injustice and discrimination. He reigns supreme over the other orishas who must count with his blessing for all their undertakings. He is the staunchest ally a person can have and the most formidable foe. Through him all things are possible for he has in his hands the power of Olodumare.

EBBÓS

An Ebbó is an offering to an orisha for the purpose of acquiring his ashé. This ashé is cosmic power which can be manipulated in many ways to accomplish what is desired. Each orisha has his/her own ebbós which are given to propitiate his/her aid in a given problem. With Eleggua, as with all the other orishas, the preparation of the offerings or ebbós must take into consideration the colors, days, numbers, attributes and favorite foods of the deities. When this information is known it is then possible to propitiate the orisha of one's choosing by creating or designing very personal ebbós, and offering them to the deity to engage his/her aid in the problem or dilemma faced by the person. Following are some of the traditional ebbós given to Eleggua for specific needs. All the ingredients can be found at the stores known as botanicas which cater to the needs of the santeros.

A Cleansing

Three eggs are covered with palm oil *(manteca de corojo)* and sprayed with rum and cigar smoke. They are then placed in a paper bag which the individual then rubs over his body — head to foot. The eggs are then crushed on three separate corners away from the person's home, asking Eleggua to cleanse away all evil influences and to break away all obstacles the same way the eggs are being broken. This is repeated during three days starting on a Monday, Eleggua's ascribed day in Santería.

For Money

Four balls are made of raw corn meal, honey, palm oil and smoked fish and possum *(pescado y jutía)*. They are then placed in the four corners of the block where the person lives, asking Eleggua for money and prosperity.

For Money

Three smoked fish *(arencas)* are covered with palm oil and placed on a small dish on the floor in front of Eleggua, asking the orisha to bring new prosperity to the house.

For Love

The name of the person is written on a piece of brown paper and placed between three stick of the following woods *(palos)*: *llamao, parami* and *vencedor*. The name and the sticks are then wrapped tightly with red and black threads. It is important that the name and the sticks are completely covered by the thread. Thus secured, they are then placed, inside a glass with rum, honey and cinnamon. The glass is placed on the floor in front of Eleggua, who is then asked to intercede and unite the two lovers.

For Good Luck

The person buys four coconuts in Eleggua's name and stands in front of the vessel holding Eleggua's image. He makes the sign of the cross with each coconut and proceeds to rub them one by one all over his body, head to foot, asking that his luck change for the better. He then takes the four coconuts to a park and places them around him in the form of a cross, which symbolizes the four cardinal points. He proceeds to break each coconut with a hammer, starting with the one facing to the east. When all are broken, he jumps over them and returns home without looking back, secure in the knowledge that his luck will soon begin to improve.

Mondays Belong to Eleggua

Mondays are Eleggua's day in Santería. The practitioners of the religion always remember to give the orisha a small dish of candies on this day, together with fresh water, rum, a cigar and a white candle. Three drops of the water are let fall on the floor in front of Eleggua's image while the person prays to the orisha. Some rum and cigar smoke are then sprayed over the image and the candle is lit. The candies of the previous week are rubbed over the person's body to cleanse him from negative vibrations and to attract sweetness to his life. The dish is then refilled with new candies and the old ones are thrown into the street.

Oggún

▼▼▼

S aint Peter is Oggún's most popular syncretism, but as in the case of Eleggua, he has many aspects and has been identified with several saints. Among these are Saint Paul, Saint John the Baptist, and Saint James. In Rio he has been identified with Saint George.

Saint Peter — Feast Day: June 29th

Peter was a fisherman in the Sea of Galilee, married and brother to Saint Andrew. Originally his name was Simon, but Jesus changed it to Kepha, which in Aramaic means "rock." Later on, the name was translated into Greek from which Peter is derived. Of him Jesus said, "Upon this rock (Peter) I will build my church," conferring upon him the keys to the kingdom of heaven. Peter was the leader of the Christian community and, together with Saint Paul, was the architect of Christianity. He was martyred under Nero and is said to have been crucified upside down at his request, as he did not consider himself worthy to die the same way as Jesus. He is believed to have been buried below the altar of the Vatican basilica, where the chains that bound him are in exhibition. Saint Peter is symbolized by two crossed keys.

OGGÚN AS A COSMIC FORCE

Oggún represents work and all human effort. He is also a symbol of violence, of brute force, of raw energy. He is one of the older orishas, brother to Eleggua, Ochosi and Changó, with whom he has had many battles. He is the divine ironworker, who toils eternally without rest. He lives in the woods which he owns.

OGGÚN'S REPRESENTATION

In Santería this orisha is envisioned as a black man, handsome and muscular, dressed in a green and black cassock and a skirt of palm fronds *(mariwó)*. He wears a large straw hat and carries a machete by his side. He is always accompanied by a black dog. He is violent and astute, dangerous and cagey. His bad temper is legendary but he is also honest and hard working. He is represented by seven work implements: a rake, a spade, a pick, a chisel, a hammer, a knife and an anvil, which are kept inside a black cauldron. In the cauldron are also placed three railway spikes, a black stone, a piece of chain and three horseshoes. He represents work and all minerals and metals, especially iron.

ATTRIBUTES

His seven iron implements, among which are: a rake, a spade, a pick, a chisel, a hammer, a knife, an anvil, and a machete. His attributes also include a straw hat, a skirt of mariwó, black dogs, a set of 18 cowrie shells for divination, a black stone, chains, horseshoes, magnets, iron filings.

Colors: Green and black

Days of the Week: Tuesday and Wednesday and the 4th of each month

Numbers: 3 and 7

Offerings: Cigars, rum, toy weapons, toy cars and airplanes.

Necklace: Alternating black and green beads, although in some of his paths, the colors may differ.

Foods: Seven plantains covered with palm oil, roasted ñame, kola nuts, white beans, roosters, goats, possum, toasted corn, palm oil, smoked fish, seven soda crackers spread with palm oil.

Herbs (in Spanish): Pata de gallina, adormidera, anamú, romerillo, yerba de la sangre, cajuela, cardosanto, algarrobo, caimito, gengibre, jaguey, maiz, palo amargo, tabaco and pimienta negra.

OGGÚN AS AN ARCHETYPE

As a human archetype Oggún is seen in people of violent tempers, always ready to start an argument or a fight, and also people who are at the mercy of their lower instincts, who can be brutal and destructive. On the positive side, Oggún is also represented in hard working people, the "workaholics," who use work as an escape as much as a way to make a living. Surgeons, engineers, policemen and farmers are also under Oggún's sphere of influence.

PATHS OF OGGÚN

Oggún Bi — This a dark and violent path, where the orisha causes all types of accidents.

Oggún Nike — Very little is known of this path.

Oggún Kubú — In this path the orisha represents all killers.

Oggún Toyé — The iron worker.

Oggún Dei — In this path he represents the farmer and the peasant.

Oggún Laiké — Very little is known of this path.

Oggún Meyi — A path where the orisha has a dual personality, one bloodthirsty and violent and the other hardworking and peaceful.

Oggún Oké — The owner of the mountains.

Oggún Chibiriki — Here the orisha is shown as jealous and violent, with a ferocity and daring unequaled on earth.

The santeros say Oggún's name is Oyó Oggún. Although the preceding are the paths with which he is most commonly identified, he has other aspects such as Oggún Onilé, where he represents landed gentry; Oggún Aguanille, owner of the woods; Oggún Valenye, the tiller of the land; and Oggún Areré, the iron worker.

INITIATION

Oggún is received together with Eleggua and Ochosi in the initiation known as Eleggua and the Warriors. As I have already explained he is presented to the initiate as seven metal implements inside a black cauldron. When a son or daughter of Oggún undergoes the initiation of the asiento and becomes a santero or santera, the mysteries of the orisha are then fully conferred upon the person during that very lengthy and complicated ceremony.

THE LEGEND/PATAKI

Oggún is king of the Yoruba city of Iré in Nigeria. For that reason he is known as Oniiré (King of Iré) and Oggún Alaakoro. Akoro is a diadem worn by the orisha, who, for unknown reasons, does not have the right to wear the crown *(Adé)*, made of colored beads which hang over the faces of the royal orishas, hiding them from view. There are many legends about the controversial Oggún, but the most popular tells the following story: Oggún was born from the depths of the earth because he represents all minerals and metal ores. His father is Obatalá and his mother is Yemmu, an early aspect of Yemayá. Because he represents unbridled instincts, he abused his mother whom he saw as just another woman. When his father discovered the outrage, Oggún recognized his sin and asked that he be allowed to curse himself. When

Obatalá acceded, Oggún swore that he would work without rest for the other orishas and for humanity until the end of time. He then went into self exile in the woods, full of bitterness and self reproach. He remained there for eons, plunging the earth into war and desolation. It took all the charm and beguiling beauty of the Venus of the Yoruba pantheon, the irresistible Oshún, to bring him back into the world and to put a stop to all the carnage and destruction unleashed by Oggún. But although Oshún succeeded in bringing Oggún out of the woods, he continues to sojourn there most of the time. Oggún is a great warrior and a powerful witch who knows all the magical uses of the herbs under his command. His wife is the beautiful and powerful Oyá, who Changó seduced and took away from Oggún in retaliation for Oggún's offense against their mother. For this reason (although there are others), Oggún and Changó are in constant battle with each other. Oggún is of paramount importance to the other orishas and to humanity because he is the one who procures their food. That is why he is known as Ochogún. His is the knife that kills all animal offers and his is the effort that keeps the woods and the earth teeming with food. His lesson is that energy can be both creative and destructive.

THE ODDU

In the Diloggún or seashell divination the oddus or patterns through which Oggún speaks are Okanasodde, Oggundá, Oddi, Ofun and Ojuani, with numbers 1, 3, 7, 10 and 11 respectively.

RULERSHIP

Oggún rules all minerals and metals and metal implements; he procures work for the unemployed and protects against accidents, surgeries and prevents tragedies, which he also causes.

EBBÓS

Before a Surgical Procedure

A new knife is wrapped in a piece of deer skin which is placed over a green handkerchief and covered with the herbs adormidera, salvadera and abre camino. Three bottles of rum are placed around the offer in the form of a triangle. Two white candles are lit in front of the offer daily during seven days, asking Oggún to help the person have a safe operation and guide the hand of the surgeon during the procedure. At the end of this time the offer is wrapped in the handkerchief, which is brought to the woods and placed underneath a large bush. The three bottles of rum are opened and poured on the ground around the bush.

To Find Employment

A large key is placed inside a small clay vessel, covered with honey, palm oil and run. It is surrounded with a circle of iron filings and seven magnets. A green, glass-encased seven-day candle is lit, asking Oggún to help the person find a job. When the candle is consumed, the key is removed from the mixture and placed inside a small green bag with the magnets. The bag is carried every time the person goes out in search of employment. The other ingredients are thrown out.

To Prevent Car Accidents

About one quarter pound of ground meat is well mixed with palm oil (manteca de corojo). The mixture is then sprayed with rum and cigar smoke and divided into six equal parts. These are then rubbed around the four tires, the front and the back of the car, asking Oggún to keep the car and its occupants safe from accidents.

Protection Against Enemies

The top of an orange is removed and the fruit is hollowed.

The name of the presumed enemy is written on a piece of brown paper and placed inside the orange with honey, rum, manteca de corojo and 11 guinea peppers *(pimienta de guinea)*. The top of the orange is then replaced and secured with three sticks of the wood (palo) known as amanza guapo. The orange is then securely wrapped with a thin chain and left in the woods underneath a bush with seven pennies. Upon returning to his house, the person then lights a green candle to Oggún, asking him to subdue the enemy. This ebbó is designed to overcome the enemy without harming him. That is why honey and manteca de corojo are used inside an orange which are symbols of softness and sweetness. The guinea peppers and the chain, on the other hand, are firm reminders that this person is to be subdued.

Ochosi

▼▼▼

As with the other orishas, Ochosi has been identified with several saints, such as Saint Albert, Saint Hubert and Saint James. The most popular syncretism, however, is that of Saint Norbert.

Saint Norbert — Feast Day: June 6th

Saint Norbert was born in Magdeburg in 1080 of a noble German family. He spent his youth leading a courtier's life. He then underwent a sudden conversion after a thunderbolt fell by his side narrowly missing him. He gave away all his worldly possessions and joined the order of Saint Augustine, spending the rest of his life as an itinerant preacher throughout France and Germany. He founded the order of Premonstratensian Canons and later became archbishop of Magdeburg. He died in 1134 and was canonized in 1582. His emblem is a monstrance, the gold chalice where the Holy Host is exposed to be worshipped by the faithful. It is most likely that in the syncretism with Ochosi, Saint Norbert has been confused with Saint Hubert, who is the patron of hunters and a natural choice as Ochosi's Catholic alter ego. Saint Hubert was a French prince of the royal blood who lived a dissolute life without a care in the world. While hunting in a forest on a Good Friday, he met a beautiful stag with a silver cross on its forehead. The stag spoke to him, exhorting him to take holy orders or burn in hell if he refused. Terrified, the young prince abandoned his previous worthless life and became a monk. He had a brilliant religious life and died in 727. In 1444, Gerard V of France instituted the Order of the Horn in his name. The necklace of the order was composed of small hunting horns. Saint Hubert is represented next to a stag and several hunting dogs. His feast day is celebrated on November 3rd.

OCHOSI AS A COSMIC FORCE

Ochosi is the divine hunter and is a representation of both divine and human justice. He works always in conjunction with Oggún, who represents brute force and the creative/destructive energies of the cosmos. Together they symbolize balanced justice, the destruction of the obsolete and the creation of new avenues of life. Their union implies the dissolution of old ties and the creation of new ones. Ochosi's hunting skills are devoted to the search for perfection, as he is constantly seeking the most beautiful and perfect creature to present to the Creator. He is a symbol of purity and idealism and is therefore the implacable foe of all that is immoral and unjust.

OCHOSI'S REPRESENTATION

This orisha is envisioned as a young, fair man, of a serene and unearthly beauty. He is dressed in violet hunting clothes and wears a hunting cap made of leopard skin topped with pheasant feathers. His knapsack is also made of leopard skin and by his side hangs a brace of pheasants. He carries a crossbow in his hands and his marksmanship is unerring. It is said that he instructs the arrow as he sends it to its destination, telling it exactly where it is to imbed itself. In Santería he is represented by a crossbow, three arrows, three dogs, a small mirror, a piece of deer horn and a fish hook, as he is also a great fisherman. These implements are kept with those of Oggún inside the black cauldron that houses them both.

ATTRIBUTES

A crossbow and everything that is related to the hunt and to fishing, including deer horns, stuffed birds and fish, and hunting trophies, and a set of 18 cowrie shells for divination.

Colors: Violet, red, green and blue

Days of the Week: Monday and Wednesday and the 4th of each month

Number: 3

Offerings: Pears, grapes, rum and cigars, palm oil, grenadine, gun powder and anisette.

Necklace: One of his necklaces has blue beads alternating with amber beads; another has green beads with coral and another has amber beads, cowrie shells and leopard fangs.

Foods: Toasted corn, corn meal with palm oil, fruits, venison, goat, male chickens, roosters, quail, pigeons, and all game birds, ball of pigeon peas with palm oil.

Herbs: The same as Oggún, pata de gallina, yerba mora, adormidera o siempreviva, anamú, romerillo, albahaca, rompezaraguey and pasote.

OCHOSI AS AN ARCHETYPE

As a human archetype Ochosi is seen in people who are quickwitted and clever, always alert, full of initiative. These people are fond of family life yet they cherish change and excitement. They are just and basically honest and unwavering in their principles. They are ambitious and love to take chances.

PATHS OF OCHOSI

His name in Santería is Ochosi Odemata. His paths are as elusive as Ochosi himself and are not common known. Among his titles are Oshode which means great witch, as Ochosi is believed to be a great master of the magical arts.

INITIATION

Ochosi is received with Eleggua and Oggún in the initiation known as Eleggua and the Warriors, which I have already described. He is also received by the initiate or yawó who is initiated into his mysteries in the ceremony of the asiento. This is one of the most complex and costly of the Santería initiations. It requires additional ceremonies that take place in the woods.

THE LEGEND/PATAKI

The cult of Ochosi is practically extinct in Nigeria, as it is said that most of the Yorubas who worshipped him were brought to the new world during the slave trade. Many scholars believe that he was at one time King of Ketu, Eleggua's place of origin. As with all the orishas, there are many patakis about the origin of Ochosi and his interrelationship with the other deities and with humanity. Ochosi is a son of Obatalá and Yemmu and brother to Eleggua and Oggún. In the beginning he had many battles with Oggún, but later they made peace and became fast friends. In his most popular pataki, he is said to have been hunting in the woods, looking for a perfect pair of quail. He had been asked by Orúnla, the diviner, to find the quail which Orúnla intended to present to Olofin. After a long search, Ochosi finally found the two birds, white as snow with circles of gold around their necks. He was elated to have captured them alive and brought them back to his hut where he secured them inside a large cage. As he still had to find other animals on consignment, he left his hut and returned to the hunt. While he was away his mother came to see him. Not finding Ochosi at home, she decided to tidy things for him while she waited for his return. The hut was small and it did not take her very long to find the two quail. She was overcome by the beauty of the birds and decided to take one for herself, sure that her son would not mind her action. She finished cleaning the hut, and noticing that it was getting late, decided to leave and return the next day to explain to Ochosi why she had taken the quail. Shortly after his mother left his house, Ochosi returned from the hunt. The first thing he did was to check on the quail. When he saw that one of them was missing, his rage knew no bounds. He ran out of his hut, trembling with fury, and shot one arrow into the air. As the arrow left the crossbow, he instructed it to find the thief who had taken his quail and bury itself in his heart. Almost instantly, he heard a shrill cry not far from where he stood, his heart stood still, because he recognized his mother's voice. Swift as the wind he flew to her side, and found her lying on a pool of blood, the quail still by her side. Filled with sorrow and regret, Ochosi cursed himself and vowed that from that day on he would be the representation of justice.

THE ODDU

In the Diloggún the oddus or patterns through which Ochosi speaks are Eyioko, Obbara and Ojuani, with numbers 2, 6 and 11 respectively.

RULERSHIP

Ochosi rules over court cases and all situations where justice is desired. He rules over jails, over judges and all lawyers. He is also the one to be invoked when someone is being victimized and wishes to chastise his tormentor.

EBBÓS

To Win A Court Case

This ebbó is recommended by the santeros for people who

face a trial where they may be imprisoned. The person buys three mouse traps, covers them with palm oil (manteca de corojo) and then rubs them all over his body, asking Ochosi to save him from prison. The mouse traps are then brought to the woods with three pennies, and a glass of rum and a cigar are offered to Ochosi.

To Overcome an Enemy

The person's name is written on a piece of paper and covered with palm oil. This paper is then pierced by one of Ochosi's arrows and placed in his cauldron, which is sprayed with rum and cigar smoke. Two white candles are lit on the floor in front of the cauldron daily during three days, asking Ochosi to do justice.

For a Special Request

A mixture of cornmeal, milk and honey and three diced pears is poured over Ochosi's symbol, the crossbow, and left there during three days. Every day, Ochosi is invoked and the request is repeated, burning two white candles in his name. At the end of the three days, the mixture is removed and the crossbow is washed and covered with palm oil.

Osain

▼▼▼

SYNCRETISM OR IDENTIFICATION: Saint Sylvester

T his orisha is also identified with Saint Anthony Abad, Saint Joseph, Saint Benito and Saint Raymond (Palo).

Saint Sylvester — Feast Day: December 31st

Sylvester was a Roman who was elected bishop of Rome to succeed Saint Miltiades in 313. Very little is known of him other than he is often mentioned in ecclesiastical history and later legends. He was eventually elected pope and died in 335.

Saint Anthony Abad — Feast Day: January 17th

This is another popular identification with Osain. Saint Anthony Abad was born in Egypt of Christian parents. Like many of the early saints, he gave away his worldly possessions to the poor and went to live in the desert, to lead a life of solitude and penance. He is said to have been gravely tempted by the devil during his sojourn there, but he was able to resist the evil lures. Later on he locked himself in a castle where he remained for twenty years. His life of routinely fasting and total chastity is credited with helping him reach the ripe old age of 105 years. He is the patron of grave diggers. His long life in the wilderness, surrounded by wild beasts, has helped his identification with Osain, a rural deity.

OSAIN AS A COSMIC FORCE

He represents the forces of nature and nature itself. All the herbs, plants, trees and flowers (ewe) are his. He is a hunter like Ochosi and a celibate deity. He is of great importance to humanity as he possesses the herbs with are the source of all medicines. All the ebbós of Santería and all the magical spells, as well as the initiations, require the power of his ewe which makes him a major figure in the practice of the religion.

OSAIN'S REPRESENTATION

This orisha is envisioned as a terrifying entity, with one arm and one leg and a huge eye in the middle of his forehead. He has one huge ear through which he hears absolutely nothing and a tiny one through which he can perceive the flutter of a butterfly twenty miles away. His mysteries are given by the santeros and the babalawos inside a hollow gourd, which is sometimes covered by many colored beads. The babalawos prepare a powerful talisman of Osain which is covered with fur and sprinkled with rum and cigar smoke. This talisman is used to attract money and general good luck. The gourd representing Osain must be hung in a high place. It is said to protect its owner against enemies. Some santeros believe Osain whistles when danger is near. Osain works with different orishas, but he usually lives and eats with Changó, partaking of all his foods.

ATTRIBUTES

All herbs and plants, rooster heads and their spurs, parrots, silver and gold coins, fish hooks and quail.

Color: Green

Day of the Week: Friday

Numbers: 6 and 7

Necklace: None

Foods: Parrots, roosters, goats and turtles

Herbs: All

OSAIN AS AN ARCHETYPE

He represents all herbalists, botanists and chemists. Those people under his direct influence are solitary, chaste and strong willed. They have a clear vision of the world and are ruled by reason, never by passion.

OSAIN'S PATHS

His name is Osain Owenewi Awaddo. Among his many titles are Osain Awushuye, Aroni and Gurunfinda. His priests are known as *Osainistas*, but do not have to be initiated as santeros. Their knowledge is the knowledge of herbs, often learned from other experienced herbalists. The Osainistas are the ones who provide the herbs required during the asiento ceremonies.

INITIATION

Osain has no initiation.

THE LEGEND/PATAKI

Osain originates in the Yoruba city of Irao which has frontiers with Dahomey. He is very closely associated with the cult of Orúnla. The most important of his patakis relate that at one time he was the sole owner of all the ewe. He was so selfish he never allowed any of the other orishas to partake of his herbs, which he kept hidden inside a gourd high on top of a tree. One day Changó complained to his paramour Oyá that Osain would not give him the herbs necessary to do one of his well-known spells. Oyá, who represents the winds, stood under the tree where the gourd was hanging and began to fan her skirts. Soon a gigantic gale was created and the gourd began to sway. A few minutes later it fell from the tree to the ground, spilling the ewe all over the forest. All the orishas came running to grab as much of the ewe as they could. That is how the herbs were distributed among the orishas. From that day onward, although Osain still claims all ewe as his own, he must share them with the other deities. Another pataki relates how Osain lost his missing limbs. According to this legend, Osain and Orúnla had been feuding for some time, and although Orúnla wanted to make peace, Osain insisted on battling with Orúnla. In desperation, Orúnla went to visit Changó, who is a renowned witch, and asked the thunder god for a spell with which he could overcome Osain. While Orúnla was consulting Changó, Osain was busy casting his own spell to destroy Orúnla. But Changó's spell proved to be the strongest. Suddenly a huge bolt of lightning fell upon the woods were Osain was hiding, setting it on fire. Trapped in the inferno, Osain was unable to escape. That is how he became lame and nearly blind for all eternity.

THE ODDU

In the Diloggún, the oddus or patterns through which Osain speaks are Offun and Eyila with numbers 10 and 12 respectively.

RULERSHIP

Osain rules nature and all natural phenomena. He is specifically invoked to protect the house and the property of the santero or the one who invokes him, and to overcome all enemies.

EBBÓS

There are no specific ebbós to propitiate Osain. Those who own his talisman simply spray it with rum and cigar smoke once a week, usually on Mondays or Fridays.

Orúnla

▼▼▼

Orúnla or Orúnmila is most commonly identified with Saint Francis of Assissi, but he is also syncretized with Saint Joseph and Saint Phillip.

Saint Francis of Assissi — Feast Day: October 4th

Francis Bernadone was born in Assissi in 1181, the son of a wealthy cloth merchant. In his youth he led a carefree, frivolous life but early bouts with civil warfare and illness sobered him up quickly. One day, while passing by a tumbled down church he heard Jesus ask him to repair his house. Francis had no money, so he sold some of his father's goods to rebuild the church. This led to his being disowned and disinherited by his father. Undaunted, Francis took off all his clothes in a public place and gave them back to his father, as they also belonged to him. From that day onward, he dressed in burlap with a rope around his waist and swore a vow of poverty and chastity for the rest of his life. Several of his old companions joined him in his new chosen path. This marked the beginning of the Friars Minor, which is the name of the Franciscan Order. The small contingent of itinerant preachers grew by leaps and bounds and when Francis dies in 1226, it was composed of thousands of devoted and idealistic young men, among whom shone like a beacon, the miraculous Saint Anthony of Padua. Two years before his death, Saint Francis developed wounds on his body corresponding to the five wounds suffered by the crucified Christ, a phenomenon known as stigmata. The wounds never healed and were a cause of great suffering until his death.

ORÚNLA AS A COSMIC FORCE

Orúnla is the symbol of wisdom. In Santería, and among the Yorubas, he is the holy diviner, the owner of the mystical oracle known as the Table of Ifá *Opón Ifá)*, with which he can see the future and find solutions to all problems, both human and divine. Orúnla is also known as Orúnmila, as well as Ifá. He is the patron of the babalawos, the high priests of Santería. He is also believed to be a great doctor with a thorough knowledge of herbs, and is said to be the one of the owners of the four winds.

ORÚNLA'S REPRESENTATION

Orúnla is envisioned as a young man, attractive and self-possessed. He is wise and infinitely patient, with an uncanny talent to see the future. He dresses in African robes in green and yellow patterns. Unlike most of the other orishas, Orúnla does not take possession of his initiates and only communicates with them through his oracles, which are the Table of Ifá and the *okuelé*.

ATTRIBUTES

They are: the Table of Ifá, which is the divining tray of the babalawo; the okuelé or divining chain; 16 *ikines* or kola nuts; a balance; a piece of elm bark; a deer's horn *(irofá)*, used to inscribe the lines of the oracle on the divining tray; the yefá or ñame powder on which the lines are inscribed; and the small broom made of horse's hair *(iruke)*, with which the babalawo cleanses away evil influences. Orúnla does not read the Diloggún, which originally was his, but he abandoned in anger when he discovered that Yemayá was reading them (better than him if the legend is to be believed). That is why Orúnla does not allow women as his priestesses.

Colors: Green and yellow

Day of the Week: Every day

Number: 16

Necklace: Alternating green and yellow beads.

Foods: Black hens and pigeons, coconuts and ñames.

Herbs (in Spanish): Albahaca, altea, colonia, corteza de coco, paraiso, copey, almorejo, aceitunillo and galán de noche.

ORÚNLA AS AN ARCHETYPE

Orúnla represents those people who are in constant search for knowledge, who are fascinated by the mysteries of the universe and are always trying to uncover them. He is also a symbol of everything that is hidden and forbidden, the incognita of destiny. All his children are shrewd judges of human nature and natural seers.

PATHS OF ORÚNLA

Only one

INITIATION

Only men can be initiated into his higher mysteries, and these are known as babalawos. The word babalawo means "father of the mysteries." To become a high priest of Orúnla it is not necessary to be a santero, although most babalawos have received the initiation of the asiento. It is said that his power is so awesome that when a man is called to be his priest, he must abandon the worship of any of the other orishas and follow Orúnla's call. The first step a man must undertake to become a babalawo is to receive the initiation known as the Hand of Orúnla, also known as *Abo*

Faca. Women can receive a similar initiation known as the *Icofá* of Orúnla, a fascinating ceremony that lasts three days. This is the highest initiation a woman is allowed to receive from Orúnla. In recent times several women have claimed to have received the major initiation of the babalawo, but this claim was later denied by the high priests who conducted the ceremonies. The secrets of the *Icofá* — which cannot be revealed by the women initiates —are kept inside a small tureen in the colors of Orúnla. During this initiation are present several babalawos, and the woman's ruling orisha is revealed by Orúnla, through the Table of Ifá.

THE ORACLES

Orúnla uses two divining methods: the Table of Ifá and the okuelé. This latter is the most common method used by the babalawo. It consists of a chain approximately sixteen inches in length, that is interspersed by eight medallions made of coconut or tortoise shell. The babalawo throws the chain on his working table and according to which sides of the medallions fall down, he writes a series of lines and zeros on a piece of paper. When he has completed four rows, he proceeds to interpret the oracle. As in the Diloggún, the okuelé may form 256 oddus or patterns. Each pattern has attached to it several legends and aphorisms which help the babalawo interpret the oddu.

The Table of Ifá is a large tray of carved wood that represents the world. Its four corners symbolize the four cardinal points and the four winds which are presided over by Orúnla, Oyá, Eleggua and Changó. The babalawo spreads some *yefa* (powdered ñame) on the tray and uses the deer horn to trace the same lines and zeros he makes when he uses the okuelé. To determine the oracle he hands some kola nuts to the inquirer who shakes them in his or her hands, lets them fall into one of the hands and then presents his closed fists to the babalawo. According to which hand the nut fall into, the priest makes the appropriate lines or zeros. This system, which is a rudimentary example of the binary system, has been used by the Yorubas for thousands of years. When the four rows are completed the babalawo interprets Orúnla's message. This method is used in special cases or during initiation rituals. When he interprets the oracles the babalawo must have his head covered with a shirred cap, similar to a cook's hat. The cap is usually white but it can also be made of gingham, in the colors of Orúnla or the babalawo's ruling orisha. This type of cap is also used by the santeros during all major ceremonies. While he is reading the oracles the babalawo must sit with his back to the wall.

THE LEGEND/PATAKI

Orúnla or Orúnmila originates in the holy city of Ilé-Ife in Nigeria, although some accounts say that he first came from a place called Oke Igeti. From there he went to Oke Itase, a hill in Ife, which was the home of Araba, the highest authority on divination matters in the system known as Ifá. There are many legends surrounding this very important orisha. One of the most popular tells how Changó was the original owner of the Table of Ifá, which had been presented to him as a gift by the Supreme Being, Olodumare. But Changó, although a powerful witch and a natural seer, was always far too busy partying and carrying on his innumerable love affairs to have much time to devote to the serious business of prophecy and divination. Orúnla, on the other hand, had received the gift of dance from Olodumare, but being of a rather philosophical turn of mind, was not very happy with his gift. Nevertheless, the gift was his and he always outshone all the other orishas during their ritual dances. This did not please Changó, whose main passion were the drums and their fiery rhythms, and who loved to show off his dancing in front of his legions of women admirers. It riled the thunder god that Orúnla was a better dancer than he. After much deliberation, he decided to approach Orúnla and ask him to exchange gifts. According to this plan, Changó would give Orúnla the divining tray and its secrets and in turn Orúnla would confer upon him the talents of the dance. Orúnla liked Changó's proposal and promptly acceded to the exchange. That is how Orúnla became the holy diviner.

Another pataki tells how Death *(Ikú)* once decided to go on a killing rampage. The whole world was filled with wails of despair as the Grim Reaper took millions of people, young and old, many of them in the best of health. Orúnla heard all these cries and decided to stop the massacre. One day, as Ikú went past Orúnla's house, the diviner stopped her and invited her to rest inside. Flattered at this request from the handsome Orúnla, Death accepted immediately. As soon as he saw that Ikú was fast asleep, Orúnla took her scythe and hid it. When Ikú awoke and found her scythe missing, she first begged and then threatened Orúnla to return it. But the diviner refused to do so until Death had agreed to stop her killing spree and to spare all those who carried Orúnla's ensign. This is a bracelet made of green and yellow beads that Orúnla's priests and initiates — both men and women — wear on their left wrists. After the pact with Orúnla, Death promised not to strike anyone wearing the bracelet unless Orúnla grants his permission. The beaded bracelet, known as Orúnla's *Idé*, is an amulet against death which can only be given by a babalawo.

ODDU

In the Diloggún, the oddus or patterns through which Orúnla speaks are Eyorosun, Obbara, Eyeunle and Mediloggún, with the numbers 4, 6, 8 and 16 respectively.

RULERSHIP

The Table of Ifá and the okuelé

EBBÓS

Orúnla's ebbós fall in the province of the babalawo who is the only one who can ordain them. When a person receives the *Icofá* (women) or the *Abofaca* (men), the babalawo always gives them a small amount of the powdered ñame known as *yefá*. This powder is said to be miraculous and is used by dipping the first two fingers into it and then pressing them in a rapid motion from the forehead to the top of the head. Orúnla is invoked to cure mental illness and potential suicides. Among the many powers of the babalawo are the ability to drive away death and to cure all sorts of illnesses. The babalawo is also empowered to conduct marriage ceremonies.

Babalú-Ayé

▼▼▼

SYNCRETISM OR IDENTIFICATION: Saint Lazarus

Babalú-Ayé is also known as Chankpanna or Soponno, his name in Dahomey (land of the Arará). Saint Lazarus is his only identification in the Catholic church.

Saint Lazarus — Feast Day: December 17th

Contrary to public belief, the Lazarus with whom Babalú-Ayé was identified is not the brother of Martha and Mary, who was resuscitated by Jesus forty days after his death. There is another Lazarus in the gospels, and Jesus tells his story in one of the many parables he used in his teachings to the apostles. This Lazarus was a beggar who hid under a rich man's table and ate of the scraps the rich man threw to his dogs. The dogs shared the few bones and bits of food with the beggar in close camaraderie. Years later, when Lazarus the beggar and the rich man died, Lazarus went to Heaven while the rich man went to hell. The rich man implored Lazarus, who sat on Abraham's lap in joy and comfort, to give him some water as he was burning with thirst, but the patriarch forbade it reminding the rich man of his evil actions and his cruelty to Lazarus when they were both alive. It is this beggar Lazarus with whom Babalú-Ayé had been identified. Like Lazarus, Babalú-Ayé is also constantly accompanied by dogs.

BABALÚ-AYÉ AS A COSMIC FORCE

Babalú-Ayé is a title that means "father of the world" and

it was given to Chankpanna, who is the dreaded god of smallpox among the Yorubas. In Santería Babalú-Ayé is perceived as the personification of all epidemics, leprosy, skin diseases, syphilis, ulcers, paralysis and all types of infirmities. Lately, the epidemic of AIDS has also been adjudicated to this orisha. Santería believes that Babalú-Ayé not only cures the illnesses he rules but can also cause them. To the santeros Babalú-Ayé is a symbol of death and illness, as well as the cure for all types of ailments.

BABALÚ-AYÉ'S REPRESENTATION

This is one of the elder orishas and is highly respected in Santería. He is envisioned as an infirm old man, with trembling limbs, his body covered with pustules. He is dressed in a short tunic of sackcloth and carries a knapsack filled with toasted corn on his left shoulder. On one hand he holds a sheaf of palm leaves and in another a staff on which he leans. This orisha is so powerful and so respected by the other deities that he is allowed to take possession of any person, regardless of his or her ruling orisha. Whenever there are sharp or disagreeable smells in a house, the santeros believe Babalú-Ayé is near.

ATTRIBUTES

Two iron dogs, a pair of crutches, noise makers, a sheaf of palm leaves tied with sackcloth and adorned with cowrie shells, white dogs with yellow spots, flies and mosquitoes.

Color: Royal purple

Day of the Week: Friday and Wednesday

Number: 17

Necklace: He has several necklaces, according to his various paths, but the most common is made of blue beads with white stripes.

Foods: All types of grains, such as rice, wheat, corn, beans, chickpeas and garbanzos, popcorn covered with palm oil, burnt bread, roast corn on the cob, green coconuts, garlic, onions, smoked fish and possum. His ascribed animals are pigeons, roosters, guinea hens and bearded goats.

Herbs (in Spanish): Cundiamor, artemisa, romero, salvia, zarzaparrilla, cardo santo, caña brava, albahaca morada, zalgazo, zazafrás, pasote, ajonjolí, bledo blanco and romerillo.

BABALÚ-AYÉ AS AN ARCHETYPE

Babalú-Ayé is identified with people with broken or missing limbs, derelicts and beggars, and those who have been abandoned or forgotten by society. His lesson is one of humility and compassion and a sense of social responsibility. He is perennially tugging at humanity's conscience, and often punishes its indifference and complacency with unexpected and unexplainable illnesses. Santería sees Babalú-Ayé in every beggar and every homeless person, and teaches that these persons must always be succored as one of them may be Babalú-Ayé himself in disguise. Those people who have masochistic tendencies or who love to parade their sorrows — real or imaginary — in the face of the world, and those who only see the darker side of things are said to reflect the negative aspect of Babalú-Ayé; while those who are always ready to sacrifice their lives and well being for the sake of others are seen as typical of the positive side of this orisha.

PATHS OF BABALÚ-AYÉ AND HIS NECKLACES

The name Babalú-Ayé means "king who owns the world." He has many paths and each one has a different necklace.

Asoyi — brown beads, 3 black and a jet bead; the pattern is repeated until the desired length is reached.

Ayano — 17 blue beads with white stripes followed by 7 red beads; pattern is repeated.

Awó — 17 blue beads with white stripes, 3 black and a jet bead; pattern is repeated.

Aliprete — 17 blue beads, 3 black, a jet bead, 17 blue beads with white stripes; pattern is repeated.

Afimalle — 17 blue beads with black stripes, 3 brown, a jet bead and 3 black; pattern is repeated.

Alwa — 17 black beads followed by a jet bead; pattern is repeated.

Bara Aribo — 7 brown beads, one black and a brown bead; pattern is repeated.

Socuta — 17 blue beads, 7 red beads with white stripes; pattern is repeated.

Lokuon — 17 brown beads, 7 blue beads with white stripes; pattern is repeated.

Azudo — 17 black beads, 7 brown beads; pattern is repeated.

Sujju — 17 red beads with white stripes, 3 black, a jet bead, 3 black; pattern is repeated.

Dacunanbo — 17 black beads with white stripes, 3 blue with white stripes, a jet bead, 3 blue with white stripes; pattern is repeated.

Nanu — 17 black beads followed by a jet bead; pattern is repeated. Tradition says that Nanu is the mother of all the various Babalú-Ayés (paths).

Afrekerte — 7 black beads, a jet bead, 7 brown, a jet bead; pattern is repeated.

Kake — 17 black beads with white stripes, a jet bead, 17 black, a jet bead; pattern is repeated.

Usunike — 17 red beads with white stripes, a jet bead; pattern is repeated.

The orisha has other titles and paths, but the preceding are the main ones. He is also known as Asowano-Asyorisha, the youngest of the Babalús. According to the santeros this is his real name.

INITIATION

The protection of Babalú-Ayé is received in a spectacular ceremony known as *Agwán*. Outsiders may be invited to be present in this ritual which is very popular in Santería, as everyone invited undergoes a thorough cleansing by the orisha. The cleansing is said to dispel illnesses and drive away death. The first part of the ceremony takes place in a separate room, sealed from non-initiates by a white sheet that is hung over the door. As soon as the rites begin every person is given a necklace of the herb known as *cundiamor*, sacred to Babalú-Ayé. This necklace must be worn for protection during the entire ritual. After the inner ceremony is finished, the sheet is removed and those waiting outside are invited to enter the ceremonial room. On the door to the room stand two santeras. One has a chicken in her hands while the other holds two eggs. As each person goes through the door, the chicken is passed over his body in a ritual cleansing, while the eggs are rubbed over his eyes. The intention is to dispel all illness and danger to the body and to the eyes. Once inside the room everyone rubs himself with a vast array of grains, diced fruits, diced meat, sugar, coffee, and other attributes of Babalú-Ayé, all of which are placed in a circle in the middle of the room. Everyone tries to cleanse himself with as many of the offerings as possible. After each cleansing the grains are thrown on a piece of sackcloth that is placed on the middle of the circle. While this communal cleansing is going on, the santeros who are present are singing Babalú's chants in Yoruba and making a deafening racket with the noise makers which are a trademark of the orisha. Some people ululate in a high pitched voice, as this is one of the ways Babalú-Ayé manifests himself. Often during the Agwán, one or more people become possessed by the orisha, who then proceeds to cleanse everyone with his *Ha*, the sheaf of palm leaves that is one of his attributes. After the ceremony, one of the santeros gathers all the discarded fruits and grains that were thrown inside the sackcloth, ties it well and carries it out of the house. Often, one of the people possessed by the orisha does the lifting of the sackcloth. This symbolizes the removal of all the ills and the evil forces that plagued those present at the Agwán. The person that undergoes this initiation receives a clay vessel that houses Babalú's mysteries. This vessel has a clay lid with seven holes. The person also receives the *Ha* and the *Cacha*, a bracelet made of sackcloth and cowrie shells with a red backing. Both the *Ha* and the *Cacha* carry within some of the powerful amulets associated with Babalú-Ayé, such as a piece of tiger skin, a rooster's spur and 16 cowries. The *Cacha* is carried for good health and protection, while the *Ha* is used for ritual cleansings.

The mysteries of Babalú-Ayé may be received also during the ceremony of the asiento by those people who are said to be his children. This is one of the rarest of the initiations of Santería, as very few people are chosen by this most powerful orisha to be his priests or priestesses. Babalú-Ayé's "fatherhood" is proven when Eleggua's cowrie shells fall in the pattern of Metanlá. This must happen during the necessary reading with the oriate which determines the ruling orisha of a person. Eleggua then must verify with the Igbo or divination aids that the person is indeed the child of Babalú-Ayé. Babalú-Ayé may be received "direct," that is, by himself, or through the orisha Oshún (*Oru* for Oshún). During the ceremony the initiate receives four *Cacha* and two *Has*. This initiation is very lengthy and very costly, as it is composed of many ceremonies. Before it begins, the godfather or initiating priest must undergo a ritual cleansing with seven large smoked fish and two white guinea hens. He must also take seven baths with romerillo, bledo blanco and cundiamor, herbs sacred to Babalú, before he can proceed with the asiento.

THE LEGEND/PATAKI

The origin of this orisha is uncertain, but it is probable that he came from the Tapa territory and later moved to Dahomey. Among the Yorubas he is known as Chankpanna, god of smallpox. In his youth he was a profligate woman chaser who had no respect for Olodumare's laws. In punishment for his dissolute ways Olodumare covered Babalú's body with sores, and made him the object of jokes and the scorn of the other orishas. Everywhere he went he was despised, and people threw water after him to show their contempt. (The santeros say that is the reason the orisha's symbols must never touch water.) Eleggua and Changó were the only ones who took pity on Babalú-Ayé. Eleggua took the unhappy orisha to see Orúnla, and the holy diviner told Babalú-Ayé he had to leave Yorubaland and go to Dahomey where he would be hailed like a king. But first he had to cleanse himself with many types of grains (that is why grains are given to Babalú). He also had to find two dogs which had to accompany him everywhere he went. Babalú-Ayé followed Orúnla's advice and underwent the cleansing. Immediately afterward Olodumare sent a purifying rain which healed Babalú's pustules. Followed by two dogs — given to him by Changó (who stole them from Oggún) — Babalú-Ayé exiled himself and went to Dahomey. As Orúnla had predicted, as soon as Babalú entered Dahomey he was proclaimed king. That is why Babalú-Ayé's color is royal purple and why he is said to come from the land of Arará (Dahomey).

THE ODDU

In the Diloggún, the oddus or patterns through which Babalú-Ayé speaks are Oddi, Ossa, Ojuani and Metanlá, with numbers 7, 9, 11 and 13 respectively.

RULERSHIP

All types of contagious illnesses, cancer, leprosy, epidemics, skin and leg ailments, paralysis and all types of infirmities.

EBBÓS

To Dispel Evil Influences and Death

The person takes 7 baths of romerillo, cundiamor and bledo blanco. As he throws the liquid slowly over his body, he rubs himself with a roasted ear of corn. At the end of the 7th day he gathers the 7 ears of corn and places them on a piece of sackcloth and pours over them honey, dry wine, and palm oil (manteca de corojo). He then blows cigar smoke over the corn, ties the sackcloth well, puts it inside a paper bag and leaves it by the front door of a cemetery with 17 cents.

A Cleansing for Good Luck

The person undergoing the cleansing places different types of grain inside a white bowl next to a large blue handkerchief. This is best done on the floor, on a place where nothing will be disturbed. Every day the person takes a fistful of the grains from the bowl, rubs it well over his body and deposits it on the blue handkerchief. He continues doing this until he has used all the grain which has been transferred to the handkerchief. He then reverses the process and starts to cleanse himself anew, returning the grains to the bowl. Finally, he cleanses himself for the third and last time, placing the grains again on the handkerchief. He then ties the handkerchief and brings it to the woods with 17 cents.

A Cleansing to Regain Good Health

The person who is ill fills a large white basin with cundiamor and places it in his bedroom. The next day he removes the basin to another room of the house. This action is continued until the basin has made the rounds of the house during 17 days. At the end of this time, the cundiamor is gathered inside a piece of sackcloth, sprayed with dry wine and cigar smoke, and brought to the woods with 17 cents.

For Money

An offering of 7 roasted ears of corn and seven bread rolls, burnt and sprinkled with salt and olive oil is placed on a white platter and left for 17 days. At the end of this time the food is brought to the woods inside a paper bag with 17 cents.

For Money

The person makes 17 balls of popcorn and sprinkles them with honey and palm oil. Two seven-day, glass-encased white candles are lit in the name of Babalú-Ayé. As soon as the candles are finished, the balls of popcorn are placed inside a paper bag and brought to the woods with 17 cents.

Aganyú-Solá

▼▼▼

SYNCRETISM OR IDENTIFICATION: Saint Christopher

Aganyú's most popular syncretism is that of Saint Christopher, but in some parts of Cuba, notably Santiago, he has been identified with the Archangel Saint Michael.

Saint Christopher — Feast Day: July 25th

There are no dates about either the birth or the death of Saint Christopher. The story that circulates in the West (the Greek story is different) is that he was a man of gigantic stature who wanted to serve the mightiest of masters. He lived alone by a ford where he earned a living by passing travelers on his shoulders across the waters. One day a child appeared and asked to be carried across. Half way through the ford the child became so heavy that the giant was barely able to finish the crossing. When Saint Christopher complained to the child about his unusual heavy weight, the child told him that the heaviness he felt was the weight of the world that he was carrying on his shoulders. The child then revealed himself as the Jesus Christ, whereupon Saint Christopher fell down on his knees and declared that he had finally found the master he was seeking. His new found faith cost Saint Christopher his life and he died a martyr's death. It is surmised that he was executed in Asia Minor in the third century. He was canonized during the Middle Ages at a time when he was highly revered and many frescoes depicting him were painted on church walls. The first church in his honor was erected in the year 450 AD. He is the patron of travelers and of the city of Havana.

AGANYÚ AS A COSMIC FORCE

This orisha is a symbol of all earth forces, particularly the center of the earth and the volcano. He is responsible for earthquakes and all the cataclysmic upheavals that change the face of the planet. Volcanic lava is seen as his fiery breath and his power is the impulse that makes the earth gyrate upon its axis. His refuge is the palm tree which he shares with Changó, who, according to some legends, is his son. Other patakis claim that both Aganyú and Changó are the children of Obatalá. Aganyú is perceived as the universal fire, the boiling core of the earth and the volcanic eruptions which give birth to new land masses and mountain ranges. According to one of the legends, his mother is Oroina, who is the center of the earth. He also manifests as the sun, although the name of the sun in Santería is Olorún. Aganyú as the sun represents the solar energy that makes possible all life on earth. For this reason Aganyú is seen as the initiation of the history of humanity and as the beginning and the end of all living things.

AGANYÚ'S REPRESENTATION

Santería envisions Aganyú as a huge man, wild and untamed, of a fiery temper. He dresses in breeches and a short jacket in dark red. Around his waist he carries nine handkerchiefs in different colors and a skirt of mariwó (palm fronds). He is said to walk stealthily with very long and measured steps.

ATTRIBUTES

Two small bull horns *(Owe)*; a red and white double-edged ax, made of wood and ornamented with yellow, red and blue beads *(Oshé)*; and 16 round stones *(Mate)* which must be taken from the seaside. Sometimes the Oshé is covered in blue beads with brown stripes. He also carries a staff covered with colored beads and cowrie shells. Among his attributes are 18 cowrie shells used for divination.

Color: Red

Day of the Week: Wednesday and the 16th of each month

Necklace: He has several, according to his paths, but the most common is made of blue beads with brown stripes.

Foods: Nine crackers covered with palm oil; nine green plantains, also covered with palm oil; eggplants and fruits of all types. Among his sacred animals are bulls, goats, roosters and guinea hens.

Herbs (in Spanish): Zarzaparrilla, paraiso, álamo, jobo, marpacífico, curey, bledo punzó, baria and moco de pavo.

AGANYÚ AS AN ARCHETYPE

This orisha is said to manifest in men of violent and harsh tempers, of powerful physiques. Gentility and softness usually disarms them, and they are fond of small children.

PATHS OF AGANYÚ

His name is Aganyú Solá Kiniba, but he is also known as Babadina (Father of Fire), Aggayú Larí and as Aggari, which is one of his oldest paths.

INITIATION

Aganyú's mysteries are received only by those people who are said to be his children. This is determined with Eleggua's Diloggún or cowrie shells. The oddu that confirms Aganyú as a person's father is Ocana Meyi (when this pattern appears twice in a row). Most santeros believe that an initiate should only receive Aganyú through Changó in a ceremony that is known as *Oru* for Changó. The reason for this practice is that the santeros believe that no one can receive the fiery energies of the sun or the volcano, symbolized by Aganyú, directly on their heads. But there are some priests who claim that they know how to conduct the initiation "direct," that is, without using Changó as the channel for Aganyú's power. In order to do the "direct initiation," these santeros say that it is necessary to sacrifice a guinea hen to Aganyú during nine consecutive days in such varied places as a well, an old house, a cemetery, a hill, a dead tree, a river, a stone wall and two different trees. During those nine days the initiate's head must be washed with a lustral bath made with almácigo leaves boiled in water. After these preliminaries, the asiento can take place. Aganyú's secrets are received by the yawó or initiate inside a clay vessel known as a *lebrillo*. This vessel has a cover and houses Aganyú's nine working implements and the black stone *(otán)* that represents the orisha.

THE LEGEND/PATAKI

Aganyú, like Changó, is said to originate in the city of Oyo. One of the most popular patakis of this orisha relates how he came to father Changó. According to the story (largely influenced by Saint Christopher's legend), Aganyú was at one time in charge of a ferry boat and he worked day and night taking people on the ferry across a wide river. One day the orisha Yemmu — an earlier aspect of Yemaya and/or Obatalá — came to the river to be ferried across. But when she tried to pay Aganyú for his services, she realized she had forgotten to bring any money with her. As she was in a hurry, she offered to lay with Aganyú in exchange for the ferry ride. The orisha, who is said to be partial to women in distress, agreed at once. As a result of this fortuitous union, Changó, the thunder god was born. Aware that Yemmu was Obatalá's wife, Aganyú knew the father of the orishas would be enraged if he discovered his wife's infidelity. Therefore he kept a safe distance between Yemmu and himself after the incident. Yemmu did not tell Obatalá about her tryst with Aganyú and when Changó was born, the elder orisha assumed the child was his. But rumors began to circulate about Yemmu's treachery and soon Changó found himself to be the center of ridicule and derision. With his usual directness, he confronted his mother with the circulating tales and she finally admitted that Aganyú was Changó's real father. By this time Obatalá had learned the truth, but with his usual nobility and compassion he forgave Yemmu. Changó, however, was not so easily appeased and he finally decided — against Yemmu's advice — to go in search of his father. But Aganyú was not willing to admit his paternity, and when Changó faced him with the truth, he became so furious that he erupted violently and a stream of fiery lava came rushing out of his mouth. The lava enveloped Changó and catapulted him towards the sky, directly into the arms of Olodumare himself. Being the son of the volcano, Changó was impervious to its fire and was not harmed by it. Olodumare was charmed by the beautiful child and, taking pity on him, gave him to Yemayá as her adopted son. Many years later, when Changó reached manhood, he and Aganyú finally made peace, and the god of the volcano recognized Changó as his son. Some santeros dispute this pataki, contending that Aganyú is Changó's older brother and that they are both the sons of Obatalá and Yemmu.

THE ODDU

In the Diloggún, the oddus of patterns through which Aganyú speaks are Okana, Oggunda and Ossa, with numbers 1, 3 and 9 respectively.

RULERSHIP

Aganyú rules fevers and high blood pressure and automobile accidents.

EBBÓS

Cleansing to Dispel Illness and Evil

Twelve pieces of okra are finely diced and placed inside a large basin filled with lukewarm water. The water is stirred with the hand until the thick substance produced by the okra mixes well with the water. The person then wraps a bar of Castile soap in nine elm leaves and scrubs himself well with it, dipping it in the okra water. When he is well soaped he rinses himself with the liquid. When he emerges from the bath he lights two white candles to Aganyú on a white plate and asks him to drive away all evil and disease. This cleansing is repeated during nine days.

For Prosperity

The mixture of corn meal and okra is prepared, ensuring that all the seeds are removed from the okra. The mixture is cooked on a low flame for a few minutes and allowed to cool. Palm oil, honey, smoked fish and possum (powdered) are added, and a tower is formed with this mush. A small red flag is set on top of the tower which is placed on a high shelf. A white seven-day candle is lit in front of the offer in honor of Aganyú, asking his help in what is desired.

For a Special Request

Nine green plantains are well covered with palm oil and wrapped in a large piece of brown paper on which a letter to Aganyú has been written, asking what is desired. The paper is secured with red string and hung in the middle of a doorway nine days. At the end of this time the parcel is brought to the woods and left at the foot of a large tree, preferably an elm or an oak.

Changó

▼▼▼

Changó has many paths and in each path he has been syncretized with a different Catholic saint. Of all the various identifications, that of Saint Barbara is the best known, but he has also been identified with Saint Mark, Saint Elijah, Saint Expeditus, Saint George, Saint Jerome and Saint Patrick.

Saint Barbara — Feast Day: December 4th

The story of Saint Barbara is told in the book *The Golden Legend*, but there are varying accounts as to when or where she actually lived (anywhere from 235 to 313, in Egypt, Rome, Tuscany or several other places). Legend says she was the beautiful daughter of a wealthy nobleman named Dioscorus, who had her shut up in a tower to discourage the attentions of her numerous suitors. Upon discovering that she had become a Christian, he attempted to have her killed, but she was miraculously transported out of his reach. He then denounced her to the authorities who submitted her to torture. When she refused to renounce Jesus her father was ordered to kill her. This he did by beheading her with his own sword. All at once a bolt of lightning fell from Heaven and struck him, turning him to ashes. This is the source of Saint Barbara's power over thunder and lightning and her direct link with Changó's legend. The virgin martyr is the patron saint of gunners, miners and firemen. Her special symbol is a tower. In Santería Saint Barbara is depicted in three different ways:

1. The image of a lovely adolescent, dressed in white robes and a red mantle. She wears a turretted crown and a halo. In one hand she holds a golden chalice and in the other she wields a sword. At her feet is a turretted tower. This is the image accepted by the Catholic church.

2. The same image of the traditional Saint Barbara, but sitting on a rearing white horse. At her feet is a large bunch of green bananas, a basket of apples and a rooster. All of these, and the white horse, are attributes of Changó. This is the Saint Barbara who has been syncretized with the thunder god.

3. The African Saint Barbara is black and has the three tribal markings (yeza) of the Yoruba on her cheeks. She is crowned and her robes are blue and green.

CHANGÓ AS A COSMIC FORCE

This most popular orisha is seen as the symbol of fire, thunder and lightning. He is the embodiment of passion, virility and raw power. When the santeros hear thunder rumbling they say Changó is galloping across Heaven on his white horse. He also symbolizes dancing, war and all the virtues and imperfections of human nature.

CHANGÓ'S REPRESENTATION

Santería envisions Changó as a powerful man of supernatural beauty and sagacity. He is noble, hard working, courageous, a staunch friend, a great healer and a clever witch. But he is also quarrelsome, boastful, an incorrigible womanizer, gambler and consummate liar. In short, Changó is a rake, but a charming and generous one. The orisha is visualized dressed in white knee-high breeches and a red cassock embroidered with gold braid and cowrie shells. He wears a turretted crown, which in Africa and Brazil has long strings of colored beads that hang over his face, shielding it from view. Like all the other orishas, he has the three tribal yeza drawn on his cheeks. The central theme of Changó's cult is based on his power which may be creative, destructive, medicinal or moral. This power is centered in his staff *(Oshé Changó)*, which generally depicts a woman with a double-edged ax *(Edun Ara)* balanced upon her head. The ax is a symbol of Changó's thunderbolt, which is also the source of his energy. It is double edged because it can either create or destroy. As in Santería, the shrines of Changó in Oyo — the Nigerian city where his cult originated — preserve the orisha's power in his thunderstones which are said to fall down to earth when lightning strikes. This is a part of the legend which so far has not been substantiated by science which denies the phenomenon. The thunderstones, which are smooth black stones oval in shape with one pointed end, are kept inside a wooden bowl known as a *batea* which sits upon a tall mortar (pilón), known as *Odo Changó*. The thunderstones are Changó's representation in Santería. The orisha holds the staff in one hand and in the other he brandishes a wooden double-edged ax, usually made of cedar and covered with red and white beads and cowrie shells.

ATTRIBUTES

Double-edged ax, beaded or painted in red and white; the Oshé Changó, a large cup where he prepares his magic spells known as *bilongos*; a maracca or *asheré*; a sword; a dagger; a mace; a machete (all his battle implements are made of cedar wood); a pair of ram horns; a set of 18 cowrie shells for divination.

Colors: Red and white

Day of the Week: Friday and the 4th of each month

Numbers: Four and six

Necklace: Alternating red and white beads, but some of his paths call for more spectacular designs. One of the most popular is made of six red beads followed by six white ones.

Offerings: Bitter kola (orogbo) and palm oil. Among the Yoruba the orogbo are used as a divination system to speak directly with Changó. Pumpkins and pomegranates are also among Changó's offerings.

Foods: His favorite food is *amalá*, made with cornmeal and palm oil. Okra is also sacred to him and sometimes his amalá is made with twelve pieces of okra. Apples and bananas are also among the most common food offerings given to Changó. He does not accept rum, like Eleggua, Oggún and Ochosi, but he is partial to very dry, red table wine, known in Spanish as *vino tinto*. He will not accept cigars as an offering. When he takes possession of one of his initiates, he will eat — literally — the embers of any cigar that is smoked in his presence. Among his sacred animals are roosters, rams, turtles, turkeys, lambs, quail, guinea hens, and bulls.

Herbs (in Spanish): Zarzaparilla, jobo, álamo, almácigo, paraíso, quita maldición, cedro, flamboyán, laurel, corn, algarrobo, plátano, ruda, rompesaraguey and rosa de Jericó.

CHANGÓ AS AN ARCHETYPE

The people who are said to be Changó's children or who fall under the orisha's influence are energetic, passionate, of unusually bright intellect, proud and arrogant. They do not tolerate opposition to their ideas and are prone to violent explosions of anger. Men are notoriously quarrelsome and confirmed womanizers, and are fond of partying and gambling, often leading a dissolute life. These people are also extremely generous and will readily part with their possessions in order to help someone. The Changó archetypes are often highly creative and/or artistic, and rarely fail to leave a lasting impression on those who meet them.

PATHS OF CHANGÓ

The name Changó means "problem" and this orisha is said to have been born with war upon his head, symbolized by the double-edged ax. One of his main titles is Addima Addima. His best known paths are:

Olofina Kake — Changó as a child, identified with Saint Bartholomew.

Obbana — The king of the drums (añá).

Obbara — One of the oddus of the Diloggún, where Changó finds himself poor and destitute and Olodumare gifts him with several pumpkins filled with gold.

Obbalube — When Changó meets with his concubine, Oyá.

Eyee — A fierce warrior who wields a machete, a scimitar and a mace while fire and lightning rush out of his mouth.

Obakoso — The fourth king of Oyo, who according to this title did not hang himself as the legend asserts.

Alayé — The one who wields the double-edged ax and who received the fire spell from Osain.

Obbadimeyi — In this aspect Changó was crowned king twice.

Lubbeo — The one who lives on the palm tree which is his throne.

Olufina — The owner of the ceiba tree, who is a close friend of Oggún.

Alafin — King of kings, ruler of Oyo.

Oban Yoko — A rare quiet aspect of the orisha where he sits down to ponder the mysteries of the cosmos.

Ebbora — He who sits on gunpowder.

Lubbe Bara Lubbe — He who was diviner before Orúnla.

Among Changó's other aspects are Dedina, Tola or Obba Tola, Obba Bi, Okanami, Lari, Ladde, Deima, Deluami, Dezacuta Bumi and Nipa. In Dahomey he is best known as Hebioso, Alabaloke and Imalo, which is the name given to him when he is united with Oyá in the cemetery. In Dahomey they worship one of the highest aspects of Changó under the name Aggaradumi, who is said to live between two fires at the foot of a volcano. This is the aspect of Changó where he does somersaults like a ram and communicates with Oke, the mountain, when he strikes it with his lightning bolts.

INITIATION

Changó is received by his initiates in the ceremony known as asiento. During the ritual the yawó or initiate receives the mysteries of Changó inside the wooden basin known as a *batea*, which is usually made of cedar. Changó's secrets include six black stones which represent the spirit of the orisha; the orisha's weapons, which include a single-edge ax, a double-edge ax, a dagger, a machete, an arrow, and a lance; two ram or bull horns; and a set of 18 cowrie shells. After the initiation, the initiate may add several thunderstones to the *batea*. Among the Yoruba, Changó's priests — those who are possessed by the orisha during ceremonies — are known as Elegun. Women are his special priestesses and greet him every morning, raising their breasts with both hands while facing the sun.

THE LEGEND/PATAKI

There are innumerable patakis about Changó. Among the Yorubas he is said to originate in the land of Oya, where he was the fourth king. Changó was a living person, who as a king of Oyo was very violent and tyrannical and very fond of witchcraft. One day a spell he was casting on his enemies backfired and a bolt of lightning fell on his palace, killing his wives and children. Desolate, the king hung himself, causing vilification and scorn to fall upon his name. Shortly afterwards his kingdom became the target of destructive thunderstorms, and his former subjects, fearful of Changó's wrath, began chanting: "Obakoso!" (The King did not hang), upon which the phenomena ceased. This brought about the deification of the dead king, who, with time, became identified with Jakuta, a deity known as the stone thrower. Jakuta is the guardian of morality, and whenever people break Olodumare's laws he punishes them by hurling down stones of fire. Changó, the man, became identified with Jakuta, the deity who represents Olodumare's wrath. Some scholars say that Changó comes from the land of Takua where he is known as Ogodo Makuluenke Iwe-se-Adomayo. The orisha is always greeted with the cry of "Kabiesi," which means, Hail to your Majesty. In one of the legends Changó was married to Obba but left her because she cut off her ears and served them to him in his favorite soup. This repulsive action was inspired by Oyá's ill-intended advice, who wanted the thunder god for herself. Oya was married to Oggún at the time, but Changó, who hated the iron worker for his old offense to Yemmu, decided to avenge the wrong by seducing Oggún's wife. Changó's action sparked the first of the many furious battles between him and Oggún. Changó's vengeful actions against Oggún are reenacted each time a lightning bolt strikes iron.

In another legend, Changó, who is forever looking for a fight, found himself at a disadvantage with his enemies, especially Oggún, who is a formidable warrior. He went to speak with Osain, who is a great witch, and asked the sylvan deity for an invincible weapon. Osain prepared a magic gourd and gave it to Changó, instructing him to dip his fingers into the gourd and spread the substance within all over his lips each time he went to war. He also instructed Changó on how to prepare the secret potion inside the gourd. The first time Changó used the substance fire poured out of his mouth. Delighted, the thunder god continued to use Osain's gift, replenishing the ingredients each time they began to run out. That is the reason he carries the *batea* with him wherever he goes. He uses it to mix the magical potion that gives him the power of fire.

THE ODDU

In the Diloggún, the oddus or patterns through which Changó speaks are Okana, Eyorosun, Obbara, and Eyilá, with numbers 1, 4, 6 and 12 respectively. Eyilá is Changó's strongest pattern.

RULERSHIP

Fire, thunder and lightning; fireburns and fevers.

EBBÓS

For Love

Six apples are cored and the name of the one desired is placed inside each apple, which is then filled with cinnamon, honey, six cloves and mineral oil. A wick is floated over the oil and lit for one hour daily during six days, asking Changó for the love of the person desired. The apples are then brought to the woods with six pennies.

For Money

Pumpkins are a symbol of money for Changó, who was once given several of these vegetables filled with gold. To get his help in getting money, a pumpkin is filled with cornmeal boiled with water and mixed with plenty of palm oil. Over the mush are inserted six pieces of okra, points uppermost. This ebbó is offered to Changó with two white candles on a white plate. Two new candles are lit for the orisha every day during the six days. At the end of this time the pumpkin is brought to the woods with six pennies.

For a Special Request

Six green bananas are covered with palm oil, tied with a red ribbon and hung on a nail. The bananas are allowed to ripen until they rot and dry. They are then brought to the woods with the usual six pennies. This simple ebbó usually gets results before the bananas are ripe.

A Cleansing to Dispel Evil

The herbs jobo, álamo and almácigo are boiled in water with a pomegranate, cut in four pieces. The herbs are strained and allowed to cool. Honey, the white of an egg, any dry red wine are added to the liquid which is poured over the body, from the shoulders down. The bath is repeated during six nights asking Changó's protection.

Obatalá

▼▼▼

SYNCRETISM OR IDENTIFICATION: Our Lady of Mercy

L ike most of the other orishas, Obatalá has many aspects, at least 24, according to most santeros. He has been syncretized with many saints, but Our Lady of Mercy is the best known.

Our Lady of Mercy — Feast Day: September 24th

While Spain was still under siege by the Moors, one of the main concerns of every Spaniard was the rescue of the many Christians who languished in the Moorish prisons. In the early part of the 13th century, Saint Peter Nolasco saw an apparition of the Virgin Mary who urged him to institute a religious order whose sole aim was the release of the Christian prisoners. Almost simultaneously, Saint Raymund de Penafort and James I of Aragon had the same vision. They joined forces and on August 10, 1218, they founded the Order of the Captive's Redemption, under the protection of the Virgin, who they named Mary of Mercy (some church scholars translate the name from Spanish as Mary of Ransom). The worship of this aspect of the Virgin is therefore more than seven hundred years old.

OBATALÁ AS A COSMIC FORCE

This very important orisha is the father of most of the other deities. He is seen as Peace and Purity and as the creator of mankind. As Olodumare is Creator of the Macrocosmos — the Universe — so is Obatalá Creator of the Microcosmos — the

Earth. The elder orisha is also seen as the male principle and as a symbol of fatherhood and creativity.

OBATALÁ'S REPRESENTATION

As the symbol of peace Obatalá is known as the King of the White Cloth. His priests and priestesses always dress in white. In Nigeria his priests wear a white cloth draped around their waists and often wear white circles of chalk painted over their bodies. Although in some of his aspects Obatalá is represented as a young warrior, his most common representation is that of an ancient old man, dressed in white robes. In one hand he holds a staff and in the other a white horse's tail mounted on a handle covered with cowrie shells. This *iruke* is the emblem of Obatalá's royal powers and is used by the orisha to "cleanse" his followers when he takes possession of one of his initiates.

ATTRIBUTES

Obatalá's "owns" all white substances, as well as silver and platinum. He is said to rule over the bones of the body and over the brain, which he created. White doves, snails, fruits with white meat, such as coconuts, and all hills and mountain tops belong to Obatalá. Milk, cocoa butter, cascarilla (powdered egg shell) rice, ñames, yucca, cotton and white pumpkins are also among his attributes, as are ivory and all white flowers. His sacred bird is the owl, symbol of his wisdom and the chameleon is also his.

Color: White

Day of the Week: Thursday and the 8th of each month

Number: 8 and all its multiples

Necklace: His most common necklace is made of plain white beads, but in each of his paths, or aspects he has different necklaces. For example, in his aspects of Oshacriñán, Oshalufón and Ayágunna, his necklaces have a large red bead after every 24 white beads and often have cowrie shells interspersed with the beads. In his aspect of Alagüemma there is a large green crystal bead after every 24 beads; and in his aspect of Obba Moro, his necklace alternates violet crystal beads with white beads; while Oshanla's necklace has 16 beads made of ivory or mother of pearl followed by 4 brown beads. The pattern is repeated in all necklaces until the desired length is reached.

Foods: 8 meringues or a meringue tower sprinkled with silvery dust; milk or rice puddings; towers of ñame sprinkled with cocoa butter and cascarilla; all white foods; she-goats; doves; guinea hens and white hens. Obatalá will not accept alcoholic drinks of any type; neither will he accept crabs or kidney beans. His children and priests are also forbidden to partake of these foods.

Herbs (in Spanish): Albahaca, almendro, altamisa, bledo blanco, campana, altea, cebolla, higuereta, malva, maravilla, tamarindo, trébol, túa túa, tuna, yagruma, algodón, acacia, chicoria, azafrán and colonia.

OBATALÁ AS AN ARCHETYPE

Obatalá manifests his influence on persons with strong will powers, stubborn and determined. His children are usually quiet and peaceful, serene and egocentric. They are extremely intelligent, with a flair for politics and leadership. They are very patient and know how to wait for the things they want. They are also slow to anger but when they lose their tempers they explode violently and vent their fury with incisive and devastating sarcasm.

PATHS OF OBATALÁ

Santería teaches that Obatalá has 24 paths or *avatars*. In some of them the orisha manifests as a male and in others as a female. Following are some of the most important of these aspects:

Oshacriñán — This is a very ancient Obatalá, who is said to be Olofi's messenger. He lives in the mountains and is always cold. For that reason he trembles constantly. He can see what no one else can and owns the owl and the Ibeyi, who are the sacred twins and children of Obatalá and Oyá. He is said to come from the Yoruba city of Ilesha. When his followers ask him for a miracle, they must express the request presenting their backs to the orisha. He uses crutches to move about but when he become angry, he throws them away and reaches for his machete. He is syncretized as Saint Sebastian, Saint Joseph and the Crucified Christ.

Obba Moro — He is a teacher who likes to instruct the very young. He is syncretized as Saint Joachim.

Orishanlá — Also known as Oshanlá and Obanlá, this is a female aspect of the orisha who must be covered with a white sheet whenever she takes possession of one of her children. This is one of the loftier of the orisha's aspects, and during her possession her initiates display uncanny gifts of prophecy and great healing powers. This is the aspect which is identified with Our Lady of Mercy and sometimes with Saint Ann.

Ayágunna — This is a very violent aspect of the usually peaceful Obatalá, but there are good reasons for the transformation, according to one of the legends. Ayágunna is a very young Obatalá, stubborn and reckless, who rides a white horse and wields a machete and a sword. It is said that he took over the rulership of gunpowder and extended its use throughout the world. As he is king of peace, so is he king of war, but his wars are against evil and spiritual and moral depravity. He is identified with Jesus at the age of 33. His white robe has a diagonal red stripe and his necklace is made of 8 red beads and 16 white ones. The pattern is repeated until the desired length is reached.

Eyenike — In this aspect the orisha is very old but he is a warrior who guards entire cities against their enemies. When he "comes down" during the Santería rituals, the entire room has to be hung with white sheets. The person possessed must also be dressed in white clothes.

Yeku-Yeku — In some traditions this aspect is male and in others it is female. His necklace is made of white beads alternated with beads made of ivory and mother of pearl. In this aspect the orisha is very old and very patient and humble. He is syncretized with the Holy Trinity and sometimes with the crucified Christ.

Alagüemma — Also known as Agüma, this aspect is said to be the owner of the chameleon and the ceiba tree. He works with Changó and knows all his secrets. In some traditions he is syncretized with Saint Lucy and in others with the Sacred Heart of Jesus.

Talabi — This is a female aspect who, according to some santeros, likes to make believe she is deaf. She is syncretized with Saint Rita of Cassia.

Igba Ibo — Also known as Obba Iba, this is an old Obatalá who symbolizes the mind of the Supreme Being and as such is represented by the Eye of God. He hides from human eyes, and whoever does see him is blinded forever.

Obba Olofún — Also known as Osha Lufón this aspect is identified with the sun and with the Supreme Being. He was the first to use the spoken word which he later conferred upon mankind. He ordained and then allowed the practice of sex among human beings. All the other orishas obey his orders blindly, for his power is so great that by simply raising his hand his will is done. In some traditions, this aspect is that of a very ancient old woman, very small and wrinkled, who trembles with cold and old age. When this aspect of Obatalá manifests itself, the person possessed is immediately covered head to tow by a large white sheet. This aspect is syncretized as Jesus of Nazareth. During the *Tambores* or drum parties, the drum rhythms in honor of Obba Olufón are danced by bending the body down towards the floor, until the hands are almost touching the ground. The feet are shuffled, mimicking the steps of a very old person, while the dancers move slowly back and forth three times.

Baba Asho — This is not a well known aspect where the orisha is syncretized as Saint Joseph. Among his attributes are an ax, a white lily and two white doves.

Other important aspects of Obatalá are Yelu, Yemmu, Oggan, Orolu, Elefuro, Ayaluwa, Oloyo-Ocumi and Iroco.

INITIATION

The children of Obatalá receive his initiation only during the ceremony of the asiento. The initiate or yawó receives Obatalá's mysteries inside a white tureen that represents the sanctuary of every human life. The mysteries are gathered in 8 white smooth stones which are said to be the spirit of the orisha; two eggs of mother of pearl, as it is said that Olofi's heavenly palace is made of this substance; a silver half moon to represent Yemmu, Obatalá's main female aspect, as well as his wife; a silver sun, a symbol of God on earth; a silver ring, a symbol of the planet earth; a silver ficca or closed fist to represent the mountain (Oke). Together with the tureen or sopera the yawó receives a silver bell, known as an agogo, with which he can call Obatalá.

THE LEGEND/PATAKI

Obatalá is said to come from the ancient city of Ile-Ife, which according to the Yoruba myth was the first city to be created. Obatalá was not the first orisha. According to Santería tradition, the first orisha created by Olodumare was Oddudúa. His instructions were to create mankind but he became drunk with palm wine and some of the people he made were deformed, missing arms and legs. (This is why Obatalá will never drink alcohol in any form.) Seeing Oddudúa's mistake Olodumare took his spirit away and replaced it with Oddúa. Yemmu, who was Oddúa's female aspect, became his wife. Together they procreated all the other orishas. Aganyú was the oldest son and soon left his parent's home to mine the earth and illuminate it with his light (Aganyú, as we have seen, is seen as both the sun and the center of the earth, as well as the volcano). Oggún, the second son, remained at home with his other brothers and sisters. But being of an uncontrollable temper and having no respect for womanhood, he took advantage of his own mother while Oddúa was working in the fields. Eleggua, who witnessed this outrage, informed his father, who returned unexpectedly to the house and caught Oggún in the act of abusing his mother. Because Oddúa was the symbol of peace and purity, he could not punish Oggún as he deserved. In order to do so, his spirit had to leave his body and be replaced by the spirit of Obatalá in his aspect of Ayágunna. (As we have already seen this is an extremely violent aspect of Obatalá, where he is seen as a harsh young warrior.) When Obatalá/Ayágunna took over Oddúa's body, he was so enraged that the very earth shook. Terrified, Oggún asked that he be allowed to curse himself for his sin, which Obatalá/Ayágunna permitted. And even though she was the innocent victim of Oggún's brutality, Yemmu was also cursed by Obatalá who swore that every male son she had from that day onward would be immediately killed. Yemmu became so angry at these unfair punishment, that she burst asunder in two parts: that of Nana Buruku —the moon — and that of Yemayá — the ocean waters. When her next male child was born — Orúnla — Obatalá, unhappy but true to his word, ordered Eleggua to bury the baby in the woods. But Eleggua, whose tender heart trembled at the cruelty of the paternal order, decided to bury Orúnla only to the waist. The tree under which he buried the child was the ceiba (Iroko), and the tree's spirit agreed to care for Orúnla. Thus Eleggua was able to report truthfully to Obatalá that he had buried his brother in the woods. Many years later, again through Eleggua's intervention, Obatalá repented from his violent action and rejoiced at the news that Orúnla was still alive. But that is part of still another legend.

THE ODDU

In the Diloggún, the oddus or patterns through which Obatalá speaks are Oggunda, Eyerosun, Oshé, Oddí, Eyeunle, and Offún, with numbers 3, 4, 5, 7, 8 and 10 respectively.

RULERSHIP

Obatalá rules all head injuries, as well as mental illnesses which he also cures. He rules blindness and paralysis. All white things belong to him and fall also under his dominion.

EBBÓS

A Cleansing to Dispel Evil

A bath is prepared by boiling albahaca, altamisa, colonia, maravilla, malva, chicoria, altea and azucenas or white lilies. After the liquid has cooled it is strained and florida water, holy water, the milk of a coconut and the white of an egg are added to it. The person takes one of these baths on 8 consecutive nights. After each bath a white candle is lit in the name of Obatalá, asking him to rid the person of evil influences.

A Cleansing for Good Luck

The person cleans 8 coconuts and covers them, first with cocoa butter and then with cascarilla. Each coconut is rubbed over the body, head to foot, asking Obatalá to gather all negative influences unto the coconuts. These are then taken to the woods and placed in a large circle surrounding the person, who then proceeds to break them, one after the other, asking for good luck and prosperity.

For a Special Request

The request is written on a piece of brown paper which is placed underneath a white plate. On top of the plate is heaped a tower of mashed ñame, well laced with cocoa butter and sprinkled with cascarilla. The ñame is then covered with cotton, and a small white flag is placed on the top. A seven-day, glass-encased white candle is lit in front of the offer. It is said that Obatalá will grant the request long before the candle is finished.

For Peace

The name of the person with whom peace is desired is placed inside a glass of water with orange blossom water, alum and white sugar. The top of the glass is covered with cotton, asking Obatalá to bring about peace with that individual. The glass is allowed to stand as long as possible and the water is replaced as it evaporates.

Oyá

▼▼▼

SYNCRETISM OR IDENTIFICATION: Our Lady of Candlemas
(Candelaria)

Oyá is identified with several saints, such as Saint Therese
and Our Lady of Mount Carmel, but her most popular
syncretism is that of Our Lady of Candlemas, known as La
Candelaria in Spanish.

Our Lady of Candlemas — Feast Day: February 2nd

On February 2nd, the Catholic church celebrates the feast of
the Virgin Mary's purification after the birth of Jesus. According
to the Mosaic law a woman was considered to be impure during
the seven days following childbirth. After this period she had to
wait another 33 days and then bring a sacrificial offering to the
priest at the temple for her purification. This offering was usually
a young lamb or, if the woman was very poor, a pair of doves.
Because of her poverty, Mary could only offer two doves. Since the
Middle Ages, around the 5th century, the church has been cele-
brating the feast of purification with a procession where everyone
carries a lit candle. For that reason the festival is known as
Candlemas. In early times, the procession would also pay a visit
to a cemetery on its way to church. This custom is still observed
in many Latin American countries. It is for these reasons that Our
Lady of Candlemas is identified with Oyá, since the orisha, like
this aspect of the Virgin, is associated with fire and cemeteries.

OYÁ AS A COSMIC FORCE

This orisha is identified with the thunderbolt, fire and wind. She is the embodiment of all types of turbulence, and creates tempests, hurricanes and tornadoes whenever she is enraged. Unlike Changó, who represents thunder and the lightning bolt as it falls from heaven, Oyá represents the thunderbolt *(centella)*, which crackles as it zigzags across the sky. The difference between the two is that the lightning bolt falls down to earth, while the thunderbolt simply explodes with violent electrical power, spreading its energy across the sky without earthing itself on the ground. Oyá is also seen as the guardian of the gates of death, which is why she is known as the owner of the cemetery. She is not death itself, but the one who receives the souls of the dead and opens the astral doors to them. She may be seen as all the unleashed violence of nature and the destruction it leaves in its wake. Through this violence she may or may not bring death to humanity. Together, Oyá, Eleggua, Orúnla and Obatalá represent the four winds, but Oyá symbolizes the very air that we breathe. She therefore can be seen as the seed of both life and death. The santeros say that she is Olofi's "secretary" because she informs him zealously of everything that happens on earth. She is said to live by the cemetery gate or its vicinity.

OYÁ'S REPRESENTATION

This fiery orisha is envisioned as a beautiful woman with very long dark hair and skin the color of burnt copper. She is dressed in a wide skirt of nine different colors and an overskirt made of dry palm tree branches with mariwó fringes. She wears nine copper bracelets on her right arm and a multi-colored bandanna on her hair. In one hand he holds a black horse's tail with a handle ornamented with beads in 9 colors which she uses to cleanse her followers. This implement is known as *afiza*. Oyá is a warrior orisha who loves the battle. She is said to accompany Changó in all his wars and often fights with a sword in each hand.

ATTRIBUTES

The thunderbolt, the iruke, cemeteries, a skirt made of nine colors, the rainbow, the *flamboyán* tree, purple fruits and vegetables, such as eggplants and plums; flowery prints also belong to her. Her main symbol is a copper crown with 9 points, from which hang the working implements of several of the other orishas, especially Oggún and Ochosi. Among her other attributes are an ox cart, a machete and a hammer.

Colors: All colors except black; her main color is wine; she likes flowery prints which her initiates must never wear.

Day of the Week: Friday, which is chosen by the orishas to inflict punishments on those who have broken the law.

Number: 9

Necklace: Her main necklace is made of red and brown beads with white and black stripes. Among her other necklaces there is one made of violet beads with yellow stripes and another that alternates white beads with nine black beads.

Foods: White rice with eggplant and small balls made of pigeon peas. Rice with fish, rice with corn, rice with sesame seeds and rice with black beans are also among the favorite foods of Oyá, as are yams and chocolate pudding. Among her sacred animals are she-goats, pigeons, black hens and guinea hens. The ram, which is Changó's sacred animal, is odious to her, as is palm oil *(epó)*.

Herbs (in Spanish): Altamisa, cambia voz, yantén, vergonzoza, tamarindo, verbena, espanta muerto, caimito, maravilla, palo rayo, marpacífico, cimarrón, palo hacha, palo caja, granada, baria, guasimilla and meloncillo.

OYÁ AS AN ARCHETYPE

As a human archetype, Oyá manifests as very violent, quarrelsome people, authoritarian, with sensual temperaments, jealous and demanding. They are usually extremely faithful but once their affections stray, they will feel free to engage in extra marital affairs.

PATHS OF OYÁ

Among the Yorubas, Oyá is identified with the Niger river, and as such is known as Odo Oyá. Some traditions say that she originates in Oyo, like Changó. In Santeria she is also known as Yansa. In some of her paths she is known as Oyá Odo-Oyá; Oya Funká; Oya Bi; Yanza Eriri; Oyá Mimu and Oyá Obinidodo.

INITIATION

Oyá's mysteries are received by her initiates during the ceremony of the asiento inside a tureen of many colors. Among her secrets are 9 medium-sized black stones and a set of 18 cowrie shells for divination. Her initiation includes a ceremony in honor of the dead (Eggun) during which a special food known as *ajiaco* is made with the head of a pig. (Pigs are always present in the food offerings to the dead.) Nine days before the initiation the yawó must be taken to the cemetery. This visit must be repeated 9 times. In the last visit, the yawó is cleansed in front of the grave with many colored flowers. After this, two black hens must be sacrificed to Oyá in front of a flamboyán tree and in front of a wall. Only then can the ceremony of the asiento take place. Together with the tureen, the initiate receives Oyá's nine-pointed crown and her 9 copper bracelets known as *odanes*.

THE LEGEND/PATAKI

There are many legends surrounding the tumultuous Oyá. She is Changó's favorite concubine, although she shares his affections with Oshún and countless others. Some patakis claim that she is the mother of the Ibeyis or Jimaguas, the divine twins, whose father is Changó. Although she adores Changó whom she often accompanies in his many battles, she sometimes has violent encounters with him, invariably caused by his roving eye. The result of these scaramouches between the two orishas is always an impasse because their strengths are equal. The santeros say that when Changó wants Oyá to toe the mark, he shows her the head of a decapitated ram, the only object of terror for the wind goddess; likewise, when Oyá wants to frighten Changó she presents him with a skull, the one dread of the thunder god. According to one of the legends, Oyá became very curious about Changó's ability to spout fire through his mouth and nostrils. As we have seen, he acquired this power through a spell that Osain concocted for him inside a gourd. Oyá began to spy on Changó's every move in the hope of discovering the secret of his power over fire. She soon noticed that each time he went to war, the thunder god would lock himself in a room where he kept the gourd, a supply of herbs and other magical ingredients. He always came out of the room spitting fire with every word. Convinced that the secret was inside the gourd, Oyá waited until Changó had left on one of his many warmongering enterprises and stole into the room. She found the gourd in one of the far corners of the room, hidden beneath some animal hides. She immediately opened it and dipping a finger inside its contents, tasted it gingerly. It was so hot her tongue felt like burning. To ease the stinging sensation she blew some air on her tongue. All at once a gigantic volley of fire issued from her mouth setting fire to the entire room. Terrified, Oyá flew out of Changó's palace and hid herself in the woods. But it was not very long until she was found by the furious orisha who wanted to exact a severe penalty on her for having stolen his secret. Another battle took place between Oyá and Changó which again ended in an impasse. Ever since that day Oyá spouts fire like Changó and can also wield the thunderbolt. In another pataki, it is Oyá who gives Changó the secret of the fire and the lightning bolt.

THE ODDU

In the Diloggún the various oddus or patterns through which Oyá speaks are Oshé, Ossá and Ojuani with numbers 5, 9 and 11 respectively.

RULERSHIP

Oyá rules over the reincarnation of the ancestors, over memory lapses, tempests, hurricanes and tornadoes; she protects from or punishes through electrical charges, lightning and all illnesses connected with the respiratory tracts such as bronchitis and pneumonia.

EBBÓS

A Cleansing to Dispel Evil

When a person is very ill or facing severe bad luck, the santeros recommend cutting an eggplant in nine slices and placing them on a white plate. To the eggplant are added nine candies, nine bits of coconut and three white candles, each of which is cut in three parts. The person then cleanses himself by rubbing the eggplant slices all over his body, head to foot; he then follows suit with the candy, the coconut and the candles. The last cleansing is done with a bunch of colored flowers. All of these things are placed inside a bag with 9 pennies and brought outside the cemetery gates, asking Oyá to remove all illnesses or evil away from the person.

For Money

The person sews together nine handkerchiefs of nine different colors and rubs himself all over with the handkerchiefs. Nine silver coins and nine copper pennies are placed in the center of the cloth with nine magnets, dried maravilla herb, cambia voz and altamisa. The cloth is tied with 9 knots and placed on the floor. The person lights two white candles every day for 9 days in the name of Oyá, asking her for the money needed. At the end of this time the bundle is left by the cemetery gates. This ebbó is said to be especially successful in matters of inheritance.

For Money

This ebbó is prepared with a tropical fruit known as a caimito, which may be found at Latino fruit stores or ordered from one of the Caribbean islands. The fruit is sliced in half and hollowed. It is then filled with sugar, cognac and balsamo tranquilo (tranquil balm). The caimito is placed on a white dish and surrounded with 9 white candles which are lit in Oyá's name, asking the orisha for the money needed. The nine candles are repeated during nine consecutive days. At the end of this time the caimito is left with nine pennies at the front of a large tree, preferably an oak or an elm.

A Cleansing to Dispel Evil *(Despojo)*

The person takes nine baths on nine consecutive days which are made with the herbs known as cabo hacha, pasote and maravilla. Three drops of ammonia, asafetida and holy water are added to each bath. After the bath a white candle is lit in Oyá's name, asking her to cleanse the person's aura and to remove all negative influences.

Yemayá

▼▼▼

The syncretism with Our Lady of Regla is the only known identification with Yemayá in Santería.

Our Lady of Regla — Feast Day: September 7th

Around the year 1660, a small hut was erected in the village of Regla, facing the Bay of Havana. The hut was built to house an image of the Virgin of the Rule — Regla — of Saint Augustine. This venerable saint was an African bishop who lived from 360 to 436 AD. During his youth he had a vision of an angel who told him to carve the image of the Virgin on a piece of wood and to place her on his altar. The image that Saint Augustine carved was black like himself and dressed in white and blue robes with a half moon at her feet. It is this image, carved by this great saint, who is one of the doctors of the church and author of the famous "Confessions," that is honored today as Our Lady of Regla. The Virgin made her way from Africa to Spain across the strait of Gibraltar through the efforts of one of Saint Augustine's disciples, called Ciprian, who did not want her to be desecrated by the infidels. The image arrived at the port of Cadiz, after surviving intact a severe storm at sea and soon a chapel was built in her name in the town of Chipiona. Eventually she was to become the patron of all sailors and men of the sea. The Virgin is known as Our Lady of Regla because Saint Augustine and his followers lived by very strict disciplines which the saint called his "rule," a word translated as *regla* in Spanish. Thus the Virgin represents Saint Augustine's dedication to God and his strict control of his body and his mind. One of the first images that was brought to Cuba by the Spaniards was the Virgin of Regla. In 1662, the hut that had been built in her honor was torn down by a hurricane. It was not until 1664 that a chapel was built on the site and a new image of the Virgin installed there. In 1714 Our Lady of Regla was proclaimed patron of the Bay of Havana where she continues to be honored to this day.

YEMAYÁ AS A COSMIC FORCE

This beloved orisha is seen as the ocean waters and the supernal mother. She is the giver of all life and the sustenance of the world. With her help all things are possible; without her, there is only death and destruction. While Obatalá is the seed of life, it is through Yemayá that the seed germinates and manifests in many living things.

YEMAYÁ'S REPRESENTATION

Yemayá is seen as a beautiful and majestic woman, full bodied and magnificent. She dresses with the sea waves and the foam is her lace mantle. She adorns herself with pearls and seashells and the vast treasures of the sea. On one hand she holds a silver mask and on the other a serpent, dual symbol of her wisdom and her sexuality. In the *güemileres* or drum parties, she is dressed in blue and white gingham trimmed with ribbons and white lace. Her skirt must be very wide as she uses it in her dances to emulate the movement of the waves.

ATTRIBUTES

A sun, a moon, an anchor, a lifesaver, a boat, seven oars, a star and a key made of silver, lead, tin or steel. She also has among her attributes seven silver rings and an iruke — a horse's tail with a handle ornamented with white and blue beads. Her fan is made of gold and mother of pearl trimmed with beads and seashells. She has a silver bell that is used to get her attention. Many of her attributes are adorned with tiny fish, ducks, fishing nets, seahorses and seashells.

Colors: White and Blue

Day of the Week: Saturday

Number: 7 and all multiples of 7

Necklace: Her most common necklace is made of seven crystalline beads alternating with seven blue ones, but in some of her aspects her necklaces are ornamented with corals and cowrie shells, and there are many shades of blue ascribed to her.

Foods: Her favorite fruit is the watermelon, but she accepts pineapples, papayas, apples, bananas, pears and grapes. She is partial to sugar cane syrup "melao de caña", and one of her favorite offerings is a plate with seven burnt coconut balls sprinkled with melao. When the santeros want to please her they fill a blue and white plate with fried plantains and fried port rinds and put it over her open tureen. Among her sacred animals are the ram, guinea hens, roosters, pigeons, turtles, quail, parrots and ducks, although in one of her aspects she will not eat the latter. She also "eats" many types of fish. When she is very angry, the santeros refresh her with watercress, lettuce, escarole and sea weed.

Herbs (in Spanish): Verbena, mejorana, yerba buena, frescura, jugüa, maguey, yerba colonia, yerba de la niña, albahaca morada, guasima, prodigiosa, helecho, lechuga, berro, canela botón de oro, yerba mora and violeta.

YEMAYÁ AS AN ARCHETYPE

As a human archetype Yemayá manifests in very strong,

severe and willful people. They are serious and maternal (even the men), protective of the young and family-minded. These people may forgive an offense but they will never forget it. They are fond of luxuries and the finer things in life and have a decided sense of social strata. In the lesser types, the person may be arrogant and impetuous.

PATHS OF YEMAYÁ

Seven of the most popular paths of Yemayá are the following:

Yemayá Asesú — In this aspect the orisha lives in dirty or polluted waters. She accepts her offerings together with the dead and is very slow in answering the requests of her children.

Yemayá Okuti — In this aspect she lives on the breakers near the coast lines, although the santeros say she may also be found on lakes, rivers and forests. She is a fierce warrior who battles by Oggún's side, carrying his machete and his working implements hanging from her waist. She uses mice to send messages to her children. In this path Yemayá is unforgiving and harsh and is the queen of all witches. She dances with a snake draped in one arm and is said to own coral reefs and mother of pearl. In this path she does not accept ducks as a food offering.

Yemayá Konlá — She lives in the foam of the sea, wrapped in sea weed. The santeros say that in this path she likes to attach herself to the propellers of ships.

Yemayá Achaba — In this path she was married to Orúnla, who always heeds her advice in spite of their differences. She is very wise and extremely dangerous. She only listens to her children by turning her back on them. She wears a silver chain in one ankle and her eyes are mesmerizing. It is said that her magic spells are unbreakable.

Yemayá Mayalewo — In this aspect she is said to live in lakes or lagoons surrounded by wooded areas; she is a powerful witch and works closely with Oggún.

Yemayá Acuaro — This is the path where Yemayá (the ocean) meets with Oshún (the river); in this aspect she loves to dance and does not practice witchcraft. Her healing influence is used by the santeros to cure illnesses and to dispel evil spells.

Yemayá Aggana — This is an elder aspect of the orisha where she limps but walks constantly. When she dances she stoops and shuffles her feet. In Dahomey this aspect is known as Afreketé where she is said to work her magic with the aid of a snake.

Yemayá Awoyó — In this aspect the orisha wears the rainbow, known as Ochumare, as a crown. This is the oldest of her aspects and the wealthiest. She is said to wear seven skirts when she goes out to do war for her numerous offspring. She is the archetype of the perfect woman, wise, loving and honorable.

INITIATION

The initiate receives Yemayá's mysteries during the asiento inside a white tureen with blue designs. Among the emblems inside the tureen are a small siren, symbolizing her supernatural beauty; a sun, symbolizing the orisha's powers; a full moon, symbolizing her feminine qualities; a half moon, symbolizing her joy and her wisdom; a pair of oars, symbolizing the good and the evil that human beings do; a rudder, symbolizing her ability to steer humanity on the right course; and a snake, symbolizing her wisdom and her sexuality. All these emblems are made of lead which is 'the only metal that is not corroded by sea water. Also among the secrets of the tureen are seven smooth black stones and 18 cowrie shells for divination.

THE LEGEND/PATAKI

Yemayá is the greatest deity of the Yoruba pantheon because she is the mother of all that exists and of the other orishas. Even Obatalá as the father must respect Yemayá because she is not only the deity of the oceans but also the origin of earth and all of nature. She is the mother of the earth, Aganyú; of the forests, Oggún; of the flora, Osain; of the fauna, Ochosi; of the rivers, Oshún. Being water she gives birth to fire, Changó. That is why the santeros call her *Iyá Moayé*, Mother of the World. As the ocean she is also the giver of the cowrie shells which are the voices of all the orisha, including Obatalá. There are innumerable legends around this bounteous and powerful orisha. According to one of the best known, she is an aspect of Olokun, an androgynous deity who represents the depths of the ocean. In the beginning, according to this legend, Olokun reigned supreme over the vastness of the waters that lay below the heavens. With the help of Orúnla, and with Olofi's permission, Obatalá took over some of Olokun's territory transforming it into solid ground. The first land thus created was the holy city of Ile-Ife. Reluctantly, Olokun receded and let Obatalá claim some of his waters, but he is forever plotting to regain his lost domains. To keep him in check, Obatalá chained him to the bottom of the sea floor, but from time to time the awesome orisha surfaces violently in the form of tidal waves and attempts to cover the earth. Olokun is represented as half man and half fish, although sometimes the deity is also seen as a siren. Whenever he manifests he wears a mask. When Olokun was chained, Yemayá burst forth as the sea waters. The link between Yemayá and Olokun is very tenuous. Some santeros see Olokun as the mystery of the sea in its most terrifying manifestations and Yemayá as the life-giving properties of the sea waters. Yemayá always carries a mask in one hand as a subtle reminder of her hidden aspect as Olokun, and sirens are seen as her most traditional symbols.

THE ODDU

In the Diloggún, the oddus or patterns through which Yemayá speaks are Oggundá, Eyorosun, and Oddi and the numbers are 3, 4, and 7 respectively.

RULERSHIP

Yemayá rules everything that is connected with the sea or sea waters. She is the patron of sailors and fishermen and protects against drownings. She is invoked to cure pneumonia, kidney ailments or illnesses of the urinary tract. She is also the orisha invoked during pregnancies to ensure that both mother and child will be delivered safely. Yemayá also rules women and all their affairs.

EBBÓS

A Cleansing to Dispel Evil

One of the most popular of Yemayá's lustral baths is prepared by boiling seven of her herbs: yerbabuena, prodigiosa, verbena, mejorana, salgazo, frescura and colonia. The boiled liquid is allowed to cool. It is then strained and the following ingredients are added: molasses (melao de caña), sea water, seven egg whites and holy water. The bath is poured from the shoulders down and some of the liquid is used to dampen the face and the back of the neck. After the bath, two white candles are lit in the name of Yemayá, asking her intercession in removing any impure vibrations that may be surrounding the person. The same bath is repeated during seven days.

For Protection and to Attract Good Luck

The person goes to the beach, dressed in his oldest clothes. He enters the water on his left side, asking Yemayá's blessing. He makes a circle on the water with molasses and remains in the middle of this circle. He then bends down and takes some of the sea water and pours it over his head, asking Yemayá to cleanse him from all ills and to remove his bad luck. He repeats this action seven times. He drops seven pennies in the water and walks away from the sea without looking back. He goes to a dressing area, takes off his drenched clothes and puts on a brand new set of clothing in white and blue. The old clothes must be left on a trash can on the beach with seven pennies. This cleansing is said to remove all dangers and to open new roads of opportunity to the person.

For a Special Request

The person writes his wishes on seven pieces of paper. He cuts seven holes on a large watermelon and inserts the pieces of paper on the holes. The watermelon is placed on the floor on a blue handkerchief and 7 blue candles are lit in the name of Yemayá, asking her to grant the request. During seven days the person lights seven new candles repeating his invocation. At the end of this time, he ties the melon in the handkerchief and brings it to the sea. The santeros favor throwing the melon directly into the water from a boat, but some people leave the melon in a trash can on the beach.

Oshún

▼▼▼

SYNCRETISM OR IDENTIFICATION: Our Lady of La Caridad del Cobre

Oshún is identified with other Catholic saints, such as Saint Cecilia — the patron of music — but the most popular syncretism is the Virgin of La Caridad del Cobre, patron of Cuba.

Our Lady of La Caridad del Cobre — Feast Day: September 8th

The traditional story of this Virgin says that around the year 1620 two Indians known as Juan de Hoyos and Juan Moreno and a Black slave known only as Rodrigo went to the Bay of Nipe near the mining province of Cobre, to look for salt. As they were rowing in their canoe, they noticed a strange object among the waves. As they approached, they saw that what had attracted their attention was an image of the Virgin Mary that was floating on a piece of wood. The image was approximately 15 inches long, carved in wood. In one arm the Virgin held the Infant Jesus and on the other a cross of gold. The legend at her feet read: *Yo Soy La Virgen de La Caridad* (I am the Virgin of Charity). The three men, who were to become known in Cuban history as *Los Tres Juanes* (the three Juans), picked up the image and brought it to the town of Varajagua near the province of Santiago, where a small chapel was built in her honor. On May 10, 1916, Pope Benedict XV declared her patron of Cuba. The many miracles of "La Caridad" are counted in the millions. Some writers of the late 19th century described the splendor of the image. By this time, a portable throne had been erected in her honor ornamented with gold, silver, ivory and mother of pearl. The throne was surrounded by twelve angels, equally magnificent, each of which carried a golden censor in its hand. The image of the Virgin wore a crown of diamonds and a diamond pendant with an exquisite cross of the purest emeralds. She was also adorned with diamond rings and bracelets and her mantle was studded with gold filigree and precious stones. The syncretism between Oshún and La Caridad grew because of the connection made by the slaves between Oshún — who is the patron of gold and copper — and the Virgin, who was so richly dressed and whose temple was built near the province of Cobre, a copper mining town.

OSHÚN AS A COSMIC FORCE

Oshún is the deity of river waters and is also seen as the embodiment of love and sexuality. She is a symbol of gaiety, music, the arts and human pleasure. She represents the joy of life and is, in many ways, what makes life worth living. Oshún is the patron of gold and all wealth is hers to give. She also rules marriage and is the giver of fertility. Her influence is gentle and loving and she teaches humanity that the secret of life is love.

OSHÚN REPRESENTATION

Oshún is envisioned as a beautiful mulatto, with skin the color of copper, and long hair that she combs constantly with a tortoise shell comb. She is dressed in gold and yellow and wears many gold bracelets and chains on her arms and ankles. Her gown is ornamented with tiny mirrors, pearls, gold bells and cowrie shells. At her waist she carries a small gourd filled with honey, a subtle symbol of her sexuality. In the drum parties she dresses in white and yellow gingham, with a very wide skirt adorned with lace and many ruffles.

ATTRIBUTES

Fans, canoes, combs, mirrors, honey, cinnamon, gold, copper, jewels, champagne and all fine wines, honey cakes, pumpkins, coral reefs, gold bracelets and gold bells, river waters, lakes, springs and wells, peacock feathers and seashells.

Colors: Yellow, coral and aquamarine

Day of the Week: Saturday

Number: 5 and all multiples of 5

Necklaces: She has many necklaces, depending on her paths, but the most popular is made of alternating white and yellow beads or five white beads alternating with five yellow beads. In some of her paths her necklace has green, red amber or coral beads.

Foods: One of her favorite offers is the *ochinchín*, which is an omelet made with tiny shrimps, finely diced onions and watercress. She also loves pumpkins filled with honey, oranges, melons and all yellow fruits, lettuce, yellow rice, almonds, spinach, parsley, sweet potatoes, shell fish, and corn meal with palm oil. Among her sacred animals are roosters, yellow hens, pigeons, turtles, ducks, venison, quail, peacocks, canaries and crocodiles. Not all of these are sacrificed, some are just given as presents to the orisha.

Herbs (in Spanish): Anis, añil, yerba bruja, calahuala, canela, espinaca, llantén, verbena, mirto, yerbabuena, mejorana, botón de oro, yerba de la niña, culantrillo, lechuga, berro, vetivert, yerbaluisa, perejil, limo del río, malvaté, manzanilla, naranja, pomarrosa, rosas, olorosa, bejuco carey, canamazo dulce and vainilla.

OSHÚN AS AN ARCHETYPE

charming and pleasant people, who love music, dancing and the arts, fond of pleasures, extremely sensuous but careful of public opinion which is very important to them. They love jewelry and fine clothes, expensive perfumes and good wines. They are determined, stubborn and intent on social climbing at which they are very adept.

PATHS OF OSHÚN

Oshún is the youngest of the orishas but her sweetness and her intelligence earned her the right to have her very own color which no other orisha may share. She is also known as Yeyéo and Mamá Cachita, but her most important title in Santería is Yalodde, a Yoruba term that means "great queen." Her five main paths are:

Ibú Kolé —Identified with the vulture; this is a tenebrous aspect of the beautiful Oshún where she has fallen down on her luck and lives on the muddy streams. She is a ferocious witch who feeds only on what the vultures bring her.

Ibú Akuaro — Identified with the quail, in this path she heals the sick, is hard working and fond of doing charitable works. This is one of her most amiable aspects, where nevertheless, she is a bit of a spendthrift and loves to dance. In this path she destroys evil spells and banishes the dreaded abikú, who kills small children.

Ibú Alolodi — Identified with waterfalls and as Orúnla's lover — she sits at the bottom of the river — in the company of fish, a half moon and a star. She is very serious and disdains the dance. In this aspect she is also very deaf and must be called with a copper bell (agogó).

Ibú Yumu — Identified as both a warrior and as the gold coin; she is said to live where the river meets the sea. In this aspect she is said to be very old and deaf, spending most of her time knitting fishing nets at the bottom of the river. She is the richest of all the aspects. She only leaves the river to go to war next to Oggún or to dig graves in the cemeteries.

Ibú Añá — Identified with swamps and marshy waters; in this aspect she is a powerful witch and is the owner of the Batáa drums.

Ibú is a Lucumí term that means river. Oshún has other well-known aspects such as:

Yeyé Moro or Yeyé Kari — This is her happiest and most flirtatious aspect. She is constantly looking at herself in her pearl-studded gold mirror and carrying on the most outrageous love affairs.

Oshún Edé — In this aspect she is an elegant grand dame who loves to attend social functions and musical soirées. She is identified with the perfect hostess and the perfect wife.

Oshún Awé — In this aspect she is very closely related with the dead with whom she works. She is completely unlike the happy orisha, owner of the drums and of the dance, whose beauty maddens every man who sees her. In this path she is full of the sorrow of the grave and her clothes are dirty and unkempt.

Oshún Funké — In this aspect she is very wise and teaches many of her mysteries to her children.

Oshún is a happy orisha, who is always eager to grant the petitions of her many followers. She is slow to anger but when she has been offended, she is the most dangerous of the orishas and the most difficult to appease. When she is very angry, she laughs with a deep, sarcastic laugh that curdles the blood in the veins of those who hear her. If she is moved, she cries softly and that cry is a promise that she will grant whatever has been asked of her. For that reason, and because she has so many wonderful powers at her command, she is one of the most cherished and pampered of all the deities in the Santeria pantheon.

INITIATION

The initiate receives Oshún's mysteries inside a white tureen ornamented with yellow or gold motifs. Among her secrets are five yellow smooth stones from a river bed, a half moon, a star, a sun, five bells, two oars and five lances. Above the tureen is placed her golden crown and her five gold bracelets. In some of her aspects the tureen is replaced with a clay vessel. As Oshún Kolé her tureen also contains a machete, five needles, a mortar, five thread spools and a crown with 21 of the orisha's work implements.

THE LEGEND/PATAKI

In one of the most popular legends, Oshún (Kolé) was so poor that she only owned one white dress. Because she wanted to be clean at all times, she washed the dress every day in her own river waters. Eventually — because of the constant washing — the white dress became yellow. That is the reason why Oshún only wears yellow clothes. According to another pataki, because of her diligence in carrying out one of Olodumare's orders, he granted her the use of the color yellow as her emblem. All the other orishas must share the three colors that are used during the initiations: white, red and blue. Oshún has been the lover of all of the male orishas, except Obatalá — who is her father — and Eleggua, who is her closest friend. But undeniably, her favorite lover is the indomitable Changó. In one of the patakis, she saw Changó for the first time at a drum party and immediately fell in love with the handsome thunder god. But Changó, whose first love is the dance (the second is food), paid no attention to the river goddess. Piqued by Changó's indifference, Oshún grabbed a drum and began to play. Changó glanced at her and for the first time noticed her extraordinary beauty. Swiftly, Oshún dipped her fingers inside her gourd and spread some of her honey over Changó's lips. Overwhelmed by the honey's sweetness, which he had never tasted before, and by Oshún's beauty, Changó dropped his drum and began to dance with Oshún. That was the beginning of their eternal love affair. But although he enjoys his trysts with the irresistible Oshún, Changó is said to prefer Oyá as his paramour. Oshún, who is love, pines for Changó, who is passion; but passion has other expressions besides love, such as justice, ambition, and war. Oyá is desire unbridled, and she is elusive and mysterious. That is why she appeals more to Changó.

In still another pataki, after Changó stole Oyá from Oggún, the god of metals went to live in the woods, determined never to return to the outside world. During his absence, work and industry came to a standstill, and Olodumare sent for Oggún. But the irascible orisha refused to answer the Supreme Being's summons. One after the other all the orishas tried to convince Oggún to leave his shelter in the woods, but to no avail. Finally Oshún volunteered to try. She entered the woods in her most diaphanous gown, five yellow handkerchiefs tied around her slender waist. When she found Oggún she began to sing and dance in the most provocative fashion. At first Oggún tried to ignore her, but no one can ignore Oshún for very long, and eventually he began to draw closer. As soon as he was close enough, she dipper her fingers into her gourd she covered his lips with honey. Oggún immediately fell prey to her charms and she took advantage of his infatuation to tie her handkerchiefs around his neck. Thus tied she brought him out of the woods and into Olodumare's presence. Ever since that time Oggún is madly in love with Oshún, who allows herself to be adored by him but continues to pursue Changó.

THE ODDU

In the Diloggún, the oddus or patterns through which Oshún speaks are Oshé and Obbara, with numbers 5 and 6 respectively.

RULERSHIP

Oshún rules the lower abdomen, pregnancies and fertility. She also rules love, marriage, gold and wealth in general, as well as music and the arts. Illnesses connected with the blood, the liver, hemorrhages and the genital organs are also ruled by her.

EBBÓS

A Cleansing to Dispel Evil and Attract Love

Five baths are taken on five consecutive nights, prepared with myrtle, vervain, lettuce, lavender and patchouli. After the bath is strained, the following ingredients are added: honey, cinnamon, five egg yolks and Claret wine. Two short yellow candles are lit in Oshún's name after each bath.

For Love

A pumpkin is hollowed and the name of the person desired is written on a piece of brown paper and stuck to the bottom of the pumpkin with five fishing hooks. The pumpkin is filled with five egg yolks, honey, palm oil, cinnamon and almond oil. Over the oil are floated five wicks which are lit for one hour during five days. At the end of this time the pumpkin is covered with its top and brought to the river with 25 pennies.

For Money

A bread roll is hollowed in the center and placed on a small white and gold plate. Inside the hole are placed 25 pennies which have been recently gotten from a bank. Some milk and honey are poured inside the hole and a short yellow candle is placed within. The candle is lit and allowed to burn itself out, asking Oshún for the amount needed. A new candle is lit during five consecutive days. At the end of the five days, the roll is brought to the river with another 25 pennies.

Ibeyi

▼▼▼

SYNCRETISM OR IDENTIFICATION: Saints Cosme and Damian

The Ibeyi are also known as the *Jimaqüas* or Divine Twins. They are identified with several saints and in each syncretism they are given different African names. As Saints Cosme and Damian, they are known as Taewo and Kainde; as Saints Crispin and Crispinian, they are known as Talabi and Salako; and as Saints Justa and Rufina, they are known as Olori and Oroina. Their most popular identification is with Saints Cosme and Damian.

Saints Cosme and Damian — Feast Day: September 27th

According to the legend Cosme and Damian were twin brothers who practiced medicine without charging fees. During the early persecution of Christians they were executed for their beliefs. From the fifth century onward their cult became very extensive and the fame of the martyrs spread so quickly that they soon became known as the "holy moneyless ones." The Catholic church acknowledges that there is good evidence that there were two early martyrs bearing these names, but there is no known date about them. A feature of their cult was an adaptation of the ancient observance known as incubation, where a sick person slept in the saints' church in the hope of receiving a dream that would lead to his cure. Saints Cosme and Damian are patron saints of physicians.

THE IBEYI AS A COSMIC FORCE

They are seen as a symbol of infancy and represent childhood and the duality of life. There are several sets of Ibeyi; sometimes the twins are two boys, sometimes they are two girls and other times they are a boy and a girl. They are said to be the children of Changó and Oyá, although some traditions name Oshún as the mother. They symbolize the joy of innocence and are pampered by all the orishas, especially Yemayá who is said to have raised them. Like Changó, they live on the palm tree. They are the patrons of barbers and surgeons.

THE IBEYI'S REPRESENTATION

The baby orishas are represented as two small dolls, carved in wood and sitting on two low stools tied together with a piece of string. The male doll wears a necklace of red and white beads, symbol of Changó, while the female wears a white and blue necklace, symbol of Yemayá.

ATTRIBUTES

Two maraccas (asheré); two small drums; two sets of bells; two sets of gourds painted in white with a red thunderbolt.

Colors: Red and white for the male and blue and white for the female.

Day of the Week: Sunday

Number: 2

Necklace: Those of Changó and Yemayá.

Foods: Popcorn, all types of fruits and candies, cakes, cookies and yellow rice. Among their sacred animals are guinea hens, pigeons and chicks.

Herbs (in Spanish): Zapote, tomate, hicaco, maiz, mamoncillo and rabo de gato.

THE IBEYI AS ARCHETYPES

As human archetypes, the Ibeyi represent all children before puberty.

PATHS OF THE IBEYI

The santeros say that there is a main pair of Ibeyi, "and six more." These are:

Taebo and Kainde — Both male and the "main pair."

Araba and Ainá — Male and female, respectively; Ainá represents Changó's fire.

Olori and Oroina — Both female.

Ayaba and Alba — Both female.

Ibbo and Iwe — Both male.

Adden and Alabba — Male and female, respectively.

Alawa Akuario and Eddeu — Both male, are said to be the children of Oshún and Orúnla.

INITIATION

The Ibeyi are minor orishas and are not received during a major ceremony such as the asiento. Their mysteries are given to the initiate inside two small earthen jars known as *apotó*. Each jar has four black pebbles from the seaside and four small seashells. The stones belonging to the male Ibeyi are elongated, as a symbol of masculinity while the stones belonging to the female are round, as a symbol of femininity. Together with the two earthen jars, the initiate receives two small dolls dressed in white. A year after the initiation the male doll is dressed in red and white and the female doll in blue and white. Although the Ibeyi are so young, they are very wise and their power is awesome. Whenever a person wants to achieve the impossible, he is advised to receive the Ibeyi and to give them a party. The santeros assert that after the party whatever is desired is granted, no matter how "impossible" it may seem.

THE LEGEND/PATAKI

There are many legends surrounding the Ibeyi, but the most popular tells how at one time some of Obatalá's enemies wanted to kill him because they found his laws too severe. As Obatalá cannot eat salt, they bribed his cook to prepare his foods with salt so that the elder orisha would die. The Ibeyi had been listening to this plot and immediately ran over to Obatalá and told him what was being planned against him. They advised him to dress in red and black (Eleggua's colors) if he wanted to discover the identity of his enemies. Obatalá followed the twin's advice and was soon able to determine who was plotting his downfall. From that day onward, he gave the Ibeyi powers and made them the banner of the religion. This is the source of the Ibeyi's great influence and preponderance in the religion.

THE ODDU

In the Dilog ún the oddu or pattern in which the Ibeyi speak is Eyioko, number 2; they also speak in all "double combinations," known as "Melli" or twin, where the main oddu is repeated, such as 1-1; 2-2, and so on.

RULERSHIP

Children and their affairs; also all childhood diseases and impossible tasks. Sometimes the santeros invoke the Ibeyi to bring about union between two persons.

EBBÓS

These are usually offered of food in small twin plates, toys, and in extreme cases, parties to which many children are invited.

3

cotton
dirt
pennies

cascaria
rum

hutia
corn
fish

palm oil

coco butter

ree palm tree

block of honey

corner
of a
block

MTD TY: 5/2/10 - 5/16/10 **LY:** 5/3/09 - 5/17/09

Diff $	% Chg to LY	TY Net Sales $	LY Net Sales $	Diff $	% Chg to LY
424	17.4	32,875	29,385	3,490	11.9
(102)	(5.2)	23,475	22,031	1,444	6.6
76	105.5	1,457	1,568	(111)	(7.1)
450	112.5	7,943	5,786	2,157	37.3
2,129	121.1	78,978	66,321	12,657	19.1
212	480.7	1,966	2,053	(87)	(4.2)
831	199.4	31,174	25,260	5,914	23.4
103	6.2	40,013	33,208	6,805	20.5
(63)	(100.0)	1,028	804	224	27.9
90		169	66	102	153.6

Inle

▼▼▼

T he identification of Inle with Raphael is the most common in Santería.

Archangel Raphael — Feast Day: October 24th

Raphael means "God has Healed" and is of Chaldean origin. He was originally called Labbiel. He first appears in *The Book of Tobit*, which is part of the Canon of the Catholic church but is considered apocryphal by the Protestant churches. According to *The Book of Tobit*, Raphael accompanied Tobit's son Tobias in a journey from Nineveh to Media in search for a cure of his father's blindness. When they reached the Tigris river, a monstrous fish lunged out of the waters and tried to devour Tobias. Raphael told the youth not to be afraid but to grab hold of the fish and kill it. He then instructed Tobias to use the liver, the bile and the heart of the fish to prepare a miraculous ointment that was a panacea for all illnesses. With this ointment Tobias was able to cure his father's blindness, as well as other sick people. After this, Raphael revealed himself to Tobias as a messenger from God. Raphael is the regent of the sun, the angel of science and knowledge, as well as one of the seven angels of the Apocalypse. He belongs to at least four of the celestial orders, namely, the Seraphim, the Cherubim, the Dominions and the Powers. He is also one of ten Sephiroth of the Kabbalistic Tree of Life. But he is mostly seen as the angel of healing and has been often compared with Aesculapius, the

Greek god of medicine. He is the patron of fishermen and physicians.

INLE AS A COSMIC FORCE

The orisha is seen as patron of river waters, fishermen and doctors. He represents the fertility of the waters through which the earth bears fruit. Some authorities see him as a representation of human sustenance as he provides food in his capacity of divine fisherman, as well as healing human ills. He is an androgynous deity of unearthly beauty and a symbol of cosmic duality. In some traditions he is said to be the protector of homosexuals, perhaps because of his androgynous nature.

INLE'S REPRESENTATION

Inle is envisioned as a beautiful young man dressed in blue and yellow robes, ornamented with cowrie shells. Although he is a major orisha he is not very popular in Santería.

ATTRIBUTES

Two rings, a fish hook and a net, made of silver or any white metal; a pedestal in the form of a cross with tiny fish and snakes hanging from both arms. Two snakes are entwined around the center staff, an emblem that is clearly borrowed from the caduceus, symbol of medicine.

Colors: Blue and yellow, also aquamarine

Day of the Week: Friday and the 24th of each month

Number: 24

Necklace: Ultramarine beads alternated with corals; some sources give him a necklace of dark green beads.

Foods: Fish prepared with almond sauce, cornmeal and crushed saltine crackers, guava; oranges; balls of mashed pumpkin; watercress and lettuce; sweet potatoes; sweet wine; rum cakes; and almond oil. Among his sacred animals are white fish, white roosters, white doves and rams.

Herbs: All those sacred to Yemayá

INLE AS AN ARCHETYPE

The orisha is manifested in all serious, studious and scientifically inclined persons. These people are cautious, sensitive and discreet and can be at times cold and calculating.

PATHS OF INLE

He is known as Inle Ayayá and also as Erinle. He only has one path. He has a brother called Abbatá and is one of Oshún's closest friends.

INITIATION

Inle is usually received after a person has been initiated as a santero and is one of the residual initiations of Santería. That is, he is one of the various orishas whose mysteries have to be received by the santero after the asiento, in order to have full protection and control of his life. His secrets are received inside a blue and yellow tureen and include seven seashells of mother of pearl; three silver fish; seven black stones; a silver snake and a trident upon which is draped another snake. From each point of the trident, which is known as an Osun, hangs a silver fish. The trident is a symbol of health and wisdom. Together with Inle, the initiate receives the mysteries of two minor orishas: Aburutu and Abbatá, who are said to be nurses who work with Inle during his healings. Among the implements are also 18 cowrie shells for divination. Inle can only be received through Yemayá, who was his first lover.

THE LEGEND/PATAKI

According to the most important pataki, Inle was a beautiful youth whose main work was to fish, but who also hunted occasionally with Ochosi, one of his best friends. He also had the gift of healing. One day, while he was fishing, he saw a beautiful siren emerge from the water. She was half fish and her naked torso was draped with silver gossamer threaded with pearls. She was the most exquisite creature he had ever seen and he immediately fell in love with her. Yemayá — for the beauteous apparition was none other than the sea goddess — was also smitten with the handsome Inle and immediately invited him to follow her to her palace at the bottom of the sea. Inle was unable to resist her siren's call and gladly agreed to go with her. Yemayá took Inle to her fabulous sanctuary and for several months did nothing but revel in her love for the beautiful fisherman. So taken was she with Inle that she revealed to him all of her secrets and showed him all her incalculable treasures. She taught him the art of divination, at which she is the greatest adept, and revealed innumerable mysteries to her young lover, imbuing him with immense knowledge and wisdom. But as all good things must come to an end, so did Yemayá's love for Inle. The lovely sea queen tired so totally of her paramour that she could think of nothing else but how to get rid of him. Only one thing held her back: she had revealed too many secrets to Inle. If she sent him back to earth he could make use of his newly acquired knowledge, divesting her of her supremacy. Neither did she want the other orishas to know the extent of her riches. Since she did not want to kill Inle, she finally hit upon the perfect solution: she cut off his tongue. As soon as the deed was accomplished, she sent the helpless Inle back to earth. That is the reason why Inle cannot speak through the Diloggún and must only speak through Yemayá. That is also why it is necessary to make "Oro" to Yemayá in order to receive Inle's secrets. This story is told in the oddu 4-14 in the Diloggún.

THE ODDU

In the Diloggún Inle only speaks through Yemayá. Although he has 18 cowrie shells, they are never read on the floor like those of the other orishas. Neither can Inle be questioned through the coconut.

RULERSHIP

Fishing and the healing of all illnesses.

EBBÓS

These are mostly prepared by initiated santeros. It is said that one of the orisha's most powerful cleansings is done with a fish directly on the head of the person. This cleansing is believed to have the power to save a person's life, no matter how ill he or she may be.

Bibliography

Ajisafe, A. K. *Laws and Customs of the Yoruba People.* London, 1924.

Albertus Magnus. *The Book of Secrets.* London.

Aquinas, Thomas. *Summa Theologica.* Edited by T. Gilby, New York, 1969.

Awolalu, J. O. *Yoruba Beliefs and Sacrificial Rites.* London, 1979.

Babin, M. T. *Panorama de la Cultura Puertorriqueña.* New York, 1958.

Bascom, W. R. Ifá Divination. Indiana, 1969.

_____. *The Yoruba of Southwestern Nigeria.* New York, 1969.

Bass, R. H. *The story of Natural Religion.* New York, 1963.

Baxter, R. *The certainty of the World of the Spirits.* London, 1961.

Binder, V., et al., eds, *Modern Therapies.* New York, 1958.

Blumber, M. F. *A History of Amulets.* Edinburgh, 1887.

Breger, L. *From Instinct to Identity.* New York, 1974.

Bromhall, T. A. *A Treatise of Specters.* New York, 1928.

Burland, C. A. *Myths of Life and Death.* New York, 1974.

Buxton, T. F. *The African Slave Trade.* New York, 1893.

Cabrera, L. *Contes Nègres de Cuba.* Paris, n.d.

_____. *El Monte.* Miami, 1971.

_____. *Ochún y Yemayá.* Miami, 1970.

Constant, A. *The Mysteries of Magic.* London, 1886.

Courlander, H. *Tales of Yoruba Gods and Heroes.* New York, 1973.

Dean, S. R., ed. *Psychiatry and Mysticism.* Chicago, 1979.

Dorsainvil, J. C. *Une explication philologique du voudou*. Port-au-Prince, 1924.

Eliade, M. *Rites and Symbols of Initiation*. New York, 1958.

Ellis, A. B. *The Yoruba-Speaking Peoples of the Slave Coast of Africa*. London, 1954.

Epega, D. O. *The Mystery of the Yoruba Gods*. Sagos, 1931.

_____. *The Sacred and the Profane*. New York, 1957.

Farrow, C. S. *Faith, Fancies of Yoruba Paganism*. London, 1924.

Frazer, J. *The Golden Bough*. London, 1980.

Freud, S. *Totem and Taboo*. New York, 1952.

García Cortés, J. *El Santo (La Ocha)*. Miami, 1971.

Garrido, P. *Esotería y Fervores Populares de Puerto Rico*. San Juan, 1942.

Gleason, J. *The Gods of Yorubaland*. New York, 1971.

_____. *A Recitation of Ifá*. New York, 1973.

González-Wippler, M. *Santería: African Magic in Latin America*. New York, 1973.

_____. *A Kabbalah for the Modern World. New York, 1974.*

_____ *The Complete Book of Spells, Ceremonies and Magic*. New York, 1978.

_____. *The Santería Experience*. New Jersey, 1978.

_____. *Rituals and Spells of Santería*. New York,, 1984.

_____. *The Seashells*. New York, 1985.

Graves, R. *The White Goddess*. New York, 1948.

Gross-Louis, K., et al., eds. *Literary Interpretations of Biblical Narratives*. New York, 1974.

Harwood, A. *Rx: Spiritist as needed*. New York, 1977.

Hume, D. A. *Treatise of Human Nature*. Reprint. New York, 1967.

Hurston, Z. *Voodoo Gods*. London, 1939.

Iamblichus, *De Mysteriis*. Reprint. London, 1968.

Idowu, E. B. *Olodumare: God In Yoruba Belief*. New York, 1963.

James E. O. *Origins of Sacrifice*. London, 1933.

—————. *Sacrifice and Sacrament*. London, 1962.

Johnson, S. *History of the Yorubas*. London, 1921.

Jonas, Sulfurino. *El Libro de San Cipriano*. Mexico, 1952.

Jung, C. G. *The Interpretation of Nature and the Psyche*. London, 1955.

—————. *The Structure of Dynamics of the Psyche*. New York, 1960.

—————. *Mysterium Coniunctionis*. New York, 1963.

—————. Man and His Symbols. London, 1964.

Kay, J. A. *The Nature of Christian Worship*. London, 1953.

Klein, H. S. *Slavery in the Americas*. New York, 1946.

Lachetenere, R. *Oh mío, Yemayá*. Manzanillo, Cuba, 1938.

—————. *El Sistema Religioso de los Lucumís y Otras Influencias Africanas en Cuba*. Havana, 1940.

Lévi-Strauss, C. *Totemism*. New York, 1963.

Leyel, C. F. *The Magic of Herbs*. New York, 1925.

Lucas, J. O. *The Religion of the Yorubas*. Lagos, 1948.

Malinowski, B. *Magic, Science and Religion*. New York, 1954.

Mbiti, J. S., *Concepts of God in Africa*. London, 1970.

Michaelis, S. A. Discourse of Spirits. New York, 1934.

Milburn, S. *Magic and Charms of the Ijebu Province*. London, 1932.

Montagu, A. *Man: His First Million Years*. New York, 1962.

—————. *Man's Most Dangerous Myth: The Fallacy of Race*. New York, 1974.

Oba Ecun, *Ita: Mythology of the Yoruba Religion*. Miami, n.d.

Ortiz, F. *Brujos y Santeros*. Havana, 1938.

Paracelsus. *Selected Writings*. Edited by J. Jocobi. New York, 1951.

Pierson, D. *Negroes in Brazil*. Chicago, 1942.

Progoff, I., trans. *The Cloud of Unknowing*. New York, 1957.

—————. *Jung, Synchronicity and Human Destiny*. New York, 1973.

Ramos, A. *Introdução a Anthropologia Brasileira*. Rio de Janeiro, 1943.

_____. *O Negro na Civização Brasileira*. Rio de Janeiro, 1956.

Rhine, J. B. *The Reach of the Mind*. London, 1948.

Rigaud, M. *Secrets of Voodoo*. New York, 1970.

_____. *Veve*. New York, 1976.

Ringgren, H. *Sacrifice in the Bible*. London, 1962.

Rogers, A. R. *Los Caracoles*. New York, 1973.

Rosario, J. C., and J. Carrion. *Problemas Sociales: El Negro en Haiti, Los Estados Unidos*. San Juan, Puerto Rico, 1940.

St. Clair, D. *Drums and Candle*. New York, 1971.

Simpson, G. E. *Shango Cult in Trinidad*. San Juan, Puerto Rico, 1965.

Sosa, J. J. *Popular Religiosity and Religious Syncretism: Santeria and Spiritism*. Miami, 1982.

Spinoza, B. *Ethics*. New York, 1959.

Thompson, R. F. *Voices of the Spirits*. New York, 1984.

Tylor, E. B. *Religion in Primitive Culture*. New York, 1958.

Van der Leeuw, G. *Religion in Essence and Manifestation*. New York, 1963.

Verger, P. *Flux et reflux de la traité de nègres*. Paris, 1917.

_____. *Dieux d'Afrique*. Paris, 1928.

Weyer, P. *Primitive Peoples Today*. New York, 1060.

Williams, J. J. *Voodoos and Obeahs: Phases of West Indies Witchcraft*. New York, 1933.

Wyndham, G. *Myths of Ife*. London, 1921.

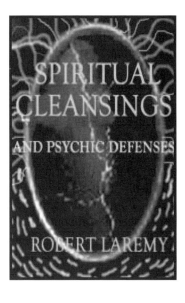

ITEM #238
$8.95

SPIRITUAL CLEANSINGS & PSYCHIC DEFENSES

By Robert Laremy

Psychic attacks are real and their effects can be devastating to the victim. Negative vibrations can be as harmful as bacteria, germs and viruses. There are time-honored methods of fighting these insidious and pernicious agents of distress. These techniques are described in this book and they can be applied by you. No special training or supernatural powers are needed to successfully employ these remedies. All of the procedures described in this book are safe and effective, follow the instructions without the slightest deviation. The cleansings provided are intended as *"over-the-counter"* prescriptions to be used by anyone being victimized by these agents of chaos.

ISBN 0-942272-72-2 5½"x 8½" 112 pages $8.95

Migene González-Wippler

RITUALS AND SPELLS
OF SANTERIA

Migene Gonzalez Wippler

Santeria is an earth religion. That is, it is a magico-religious system that has its roots in nature and natural forces. Each orisha or saint is identified with a force of nature and with a human interest or endeavor. Chango, for instance, is the god of fire, thunder and lightning, but he is also the symbol of justice and protects his followers against enemies. He also symbolizes passion and virility and is often invoked in works of seduction. Oshun, on the other hand, symbolizes river waters, love and marriage. She is essentially the archetype of joy and pleasure. Yemaya is identified with the seven seas, but is also the symbol of Motherhood and protects women in their endeavors. Eleggua symbolizes the crossroads, and is the orisha of change and destiny, the one who makes things possible or impossible. He symbolizes the balance of things. Obatala is the father, the symbol of peace and purity. Oya symbolizes the winds and is the owner of the cemetery, the watcher of the doorway between life and death. She is not death, but the awareness of its existence. Oggun is the patron of all metals, and protects farmers, carpenters, butchers, surgeons, mechanics, and all who work with or near metals. He also rules over accidents, which he often causes.

The author of this book has written "Santeria" and "Santeria Experience." This book takes us further into the practices of Santeria's followers.

ISBN 0-942272-07-2   5½"x 8½"   134 pages $9.95

Toll Free: 1 (888) OCCULT - 1

Item #039
$16.95

SANTERIA
FORMULARY & SPELLBOOK
CANDLES • HERBS• INCENSE • OILS
A GUIDE TO NATURE'S MAGIC

CARLOS MONTENEGRO

The belief in natural magic is shared by millions who are participants of the Afro Caribbean religion known as Santeria. This book was written as a *"How to"* guide for individuals who are active participants in the Santeria Religion. It's purpose is to introduce and encourage individuals of Santeria to familiarize themselves with an inexpensive way of preparing basic ingredients to produce "natural magic". Rarely is careful attention paid to the preparation of homemade magic products in these modern times. Rarer still, is finding an individual who is dedicated and competent in this aspect of spellcrafting. It is a magical institution that is dying and must not be overlooked or forgotten. Making homemade products is a lengthy process, but the success of a magical spell or ritual demands patience and faith. This book is an important resource guide to the magic found within nature. If properly utilized with respect and reverence, the Santeria practitioner will live harmoniously in nature with the Orishas.

ISBN 0-942272-52-8   5½"x 8½"

Toll Free: 1 (888) OCCULT - 1

ITEM #172
$9.95

HELPING YOURSELF WITH
MAGICKAL OILS A-Z

By Maria Solomon

The most thorough and comprehensive
workbook available on the

Magickal Powers of
Over 1000 Oils!

Easy to follow step-by-step instructions
for more than 1500
Spells, Recipes and Rituals for
Love, Money, Luck, Protection
and much more!

ISBN 0-942272-49-8 5½"x 8½" $9.95

170 PRAYERS
FOR *YOUR* SPECIFIC NEEDS
• *BIOGRAPHIES & PHOTOS OF THE SAINTS*

Original Publications

HELPING YOURSELF WITH

SELECTED PRAYERS VOLUME 2

ALLAN KARDEC

GUARDIAN ANGEL

ITEM #216
$9.95

HELPING YOURSELF WITH SELECTED PRAYERS VOLUME 2

Now With 170 Prayers!

The prayers from Volume 2 come from diverse sources. Most originated in Roman Catholicism and can still be found in one form or another on the reverse of little pocket pictures of saints, or in collections of popular prayers. Another source for these prayers is the French Spiritist movement begun in the 1800's by Allan Kardec, which has become a force in Latin America under the name Espiritismo. The third source, representing perhaps the most mystical, magical, and practical aspects of these prayers, is found among the indigenous populations where Santería has taken root.

These prayers will provide a foundation upon which you can build your faith and beliefs. It is through this faith that your prayers will be fulfilled. The devotions within these pages will help you pray consciously, vigorously, sincerely and honestly. True prayer can only come from within yourself.

ORIGINAL PUBLICATIONS

- ☐ **HELPING YOURSELF WITH SELECTED PRAYERS;** *Volume 1*; $8.95
- ☐ **HELPING YOURSELF WITH SELECTED PRAYERS:** *Volume 2*; $9.95
- ☐ **COMPLETE BOOK OF BATHS:** Robert Laremy - $8.95
- ☐ **UNHEXING AND JINX REMOVING;** by Donna Rose - $6.95
- ☐ **SUCCESS AND POWER THROUGH PSALMS;** by Donna Rose - $6.95
- ☐ **MAGICAL RITUALS FOR MONEY;** by Donna Rose - $5.95
- ☐ **MAGICAL RITUALS FOR LOVE;** by Donna Rose - $5.95
- ☐ **DREAM YOUR LUCKY LOTTERY NUMBERS;** Canizares $6.95
- ☐ **PSALM WORKBOOK:** Robert Laremy - $9.95
- ☐ **SPIRITUAL CLEANSINGS & PSYCHIC PROTECTION;** Robert Laremy $8.95
- ☐ **NEW REVISED MASTER BOOK OF CANDLEBURNING;** Gamache - $7.95
- ☐ **THE MAGIC CANDLE;** Charmaine Dey $7.95
- ☐ **NEW REV. 6&7 BKS. OF MOSES;** Wippler $12.95
- ☐ **MYSTERY OF THE LONG LOST 8,9,10TH BOOKS OF MOSES;** Gamache - $8.95
- ☐ **VOODOO & HOODOO;** by Jim Haskins - $16.95
- ☐ **COMPLETE BOOK OF VOODOO:** Robert Pelton $16.95
- ☐ **VOODOO CHARMS & TALISMANS:** Robert Pelton $9.95
- ☐ **PAPA JIM'S HERBAL MAGIC WORKBOOK;** Papa Jim - $7.95
- ☐ **HELPING YOURSELF WITH MAGICAL OILS A-Z;** Maria Solomon - $9.95
- ☐ **READING YOUR FUTURE IN THE CARDS;** Eden - $7.95
- ☐ **PROTECTION CHARMS & SPELLS;** Jade - $6.95
- ☐ **SANTERIA; AFRICAN MAGIC IN LATIN AMERICA;** Wippler $14.95
- ☐ **SANTERIA EXERIENCE;** Wippler $14.95
- ☐ **RITUALS AND SPELLS OF SANTERIA;** Wippler $9.95
- ☐ **MAGICAL HERBAL BATHS OF SANTERIA;** Carlos Montenegro $8.95
- ☐ **POWERS OF THE ORISHAS;** Wippler $9.95
- ☐ **SANTERIA FORMULARY AND SPELLBOOK;** Carlos Montenegro $16.95
- ☐ **THE BOOK ON PALO;** Raul Canizares $21.95
- ☐ **BRAZILIAN PALO PRIMER:** Robert Laremy $6.95
- ☐ **ESHU ELLEGGUA; Santeria and the Orisha of the Crossroad**; Canizares $5.95
- ☐ **SHANGO; Santeria and the Orisha of Thunder**; Canizares $5.95
- ☐ **BABALU AYE; Santeria and the Lord of Pestilence;** Canizares $5.95
- ☐ **OSHUN: Santeria and the Orisha of Love;** Canizares $5.95
- ☐ **OGUN: Santeria and the Warrior Orisha of Iron;** Canizares $5.95
- ☐ **OYA: Santeria and the Orisha of Storms;** Canizares $5.95
- ☐ **YEMAYA: Santeria and the Orisha of the Seven Seas**; Canizares $5.95
- ☐ **ORUNLA: Santeria and the Orisha of Divination**; Canizares $5.95
- ☐ **OSANYIN: Santeria and the Orisha of Lord of Plants;** Canizares $5.95
- ☐ **OBATALA: Santeria and the White Robed King of the Orisha**; Canizares $5.95

NAME _____   TELEPHONE _____

ADDRESS _____

CITY _____ STATE _____ ZIP _____